Terrorism, Jihad, and the Bible

﹡

A Response to the Terrorist Attacks

JOHN MACARTHUR

This book belongs to

W PUBLISHING GROUP™

www.wpublishinggroup.com

A Division of Thomas Nelson, Inc.
www.ThomasNelson.com

Contents

One

The Bible's teaching about sin and the human condition plainly reveals that the human heart is exceedingly wicked, capable of horrendous acts of evil. And the Bible assures us that God is still in control, and He will ultimately defeat evildoers and put an end to evil forever. There is great reason to hope and trust in God, even in the midst of so much uncertainty and strife.

One

A Response to the Terrorist Attacks

TUESDAY, SEPTEMBER 11, 2001, saw the deadliest assault ever made on American soil. With an unprecedented series of coordinated terrorist strikes on the World Trade Center in New York and the Pentagon in Washington, our lives were changed forever. The surprise attacks caused death and devastation of such monumental proportions that the attack on Pearl Harbor is the only obvious comparison. But to set the enormity of the terrorist attack in perspective, remember that about twenty-four hundred people were killed at Pearl Harbor, most of whom were military personnel. When officials are through counting the dead from the terrorist attacks, the number of civilian fatalities alone will likely more than double the death toll at Pearl Harbor. By comparison, American fatalities during the entire Revolutionary War numbered only 4,435. In fact, September 11 may turn out to have been the bloodiest day in our nation's history, surpassing even the bloodiest battles of the Civil War.[1]

The images of September 11, 2001, are imbedded deeply in our minds and will remain forever. It was a day the world, much less Americans, will never forget.

Unlike Pearl Harbor, these attacks were perpetrated not by a nation, not by a group of enemy governments and their war machines, but by a clandestine group of itinerant terrorists from the Middle East.

We watched as the horror unfolded in real time. In this media-dominated age we don't lack for visual images or verbal explanations. Four American domestic airliners headed from the east coast to the west coast were hijacked and flown on a collision course to specific targets. The intention was to kill massive numbers of people, paralyzing the nation, devastating the economy, and crippling our defense systems. The idea? To show America that our society was vulnerable. An extremist, Islamic, suicidal group of murderers was asserting itself as more powerful than a superpower nation.

Two of the planes, flying with full fuel, hit their targets with catastrophically destructive accuracy, slamming full force into the World Trade Center twin towers in New York City and causing them to plummet to the ground. One airliner hit the Pentagon, killing more than a hundred people and leaving a gaping wound in that symbol of American military might. A fourth airliner never reached its target, whatever that might have been, because of the heroic intervention of some passengers. The details of *what* happened are well known and have dominated the media ever since.

But our minds cry out to know *why* it happened. That is the natural and inevitable question.

Immediately after the initial coverage of the catastrophe, the airwaves were filled with analysts, psychologists, criminologists, and Middle East experts, who were trying to find a way to explain *why* this had happened. What motivates people to do these kinds of things? What evil sickness makes human beings capable of such atrocities? And the inevitable question that seems so out of place coming from our secular media, which normally has little time for God: Why would God permit such a thing to happen?

There are clear, biblical answers to those questions. As a matter of fact, Scripture speaks with great clarity about the evil that men do. Biblical history, going all the way back to Old Testament times, explains the roots of the political and religious conflicts that drive Islamic terrorists. The Bible's teaching about sin and the human condition plainly reveals that the human heart is exceedingly wicked, capable of horrendous acts of evil. And the Bible assures us that God is still in control, and He will ultimately defeat evildoers and put an end to evil forever. There is great reason to hope and trust in God, even in the midst of so much uncertainty and strife. Together, let's examine some of these issues from a biblical perspective.

Two

The historical reason for the terrorist action is clear: It stems from tensions rooted in biblical history, dating back to the time of Abraham.

Two

Who Is Behind These Atrocities, and Why?

THE CULPRITS BEHIND THE SEPTEMBER 11 EVENTS have become well known to the world. We now know that a highly developed, sophisticated group of terrorists in the Middle East deliberately planned and executed these heinous acts for their own political and religious reasons. Intelligence sources indicate that the direct responsibility for these events lies with an international network of terrorists headed by one person, Osama bin Laden. His name has become familiar to us as the one who probably sponsored the suicide hijackers and trained those who planned and coordinated the events. He seems to be backed by influential rulers, such as Iraq's Saddam Hussein and a large coterie of Middle Eastern Islamic extremists, including the ruling cabal in Afghanistan, the Taliban.[1] The FBI has recently released a list of Most Wanted Terrorists, all of whom are Islamic extremists. And numerous others in the Middle East are thought to be part of this massive terror network.

In other words, the terror stems from the land of the Bible. The terrorists who attacked us were not Norwegian, Argentinian, Mexican, German, or Chinese. They were Middle Easterners from the land of the Bible.

A Reuters news release issued from London days after the attack said,

> Saudi dissident Osama bin Laden warned three weeks ago that he and his followers would carry out an unprecedented attack on U.S. interests for its support of Israel. . . .
>
> Abdel-Bari Atwan, editor of the London-based *al-Quds al-Arabi*, an Arabic-language weekly news magazine, said Islamic fundamentalists led by bin Laden were "almost certainly" behind the attack of the World Trade Center in New York.
>
> "It is most likely the work of Islamic fundamentalists. Osama bin Laden warned three weeks ago that he would attack American interests in an unprecedented attack, a very big one," Atwan told Reuters.

Who Is Behind These Atrocities, and Why?

"Personally, we received information that he planned very, very big attacks against American interests. We received several warnings like this. We did not take it so seriously, preferring to see what would happen before reporting it."[2]

Who is this man, Osama bin Laden? What is this network of terrorists, and what motivates them to perform such unthinkable acts?

The same group tried to bring down the World Trade Center towers with a massive truck bomb on February 26, 1993. Their design was to topple one tower into another and bring them both down, and they narrowly missed achieving success in that diabolical mission. On that occasion, six people were killed and thousands were injured.

Since that time, the same group has been responsible for terrorist bomb attacks against American embassies, American military barracks, and American forces in the Middle East and other places. For example, bin Laden's group was responsible for simultaneous bombings of the American embassies in Tanzania and Kenya on August 7, 1998. Those bombings killed at least 213 in Kenya and 11 in Tanzania. The same group bombed the USS Cole, a naval destroyer, while it was refueling in Yemen on October 12, 2000. That attack killed 17 American naval personnel and injured 38 others. All of those attacks employed suicide bombers.

Suicide bombers from Islamic extremist organizations have lately become familiar in international headlines. Fanatics with bombs strapped to their bodies have detonated their payloads in pizza parlors, at bus stops, and on city streets with increasing frequency in Israel. In the year prior to the September 11 incident, an average of one suicide bomber every two weeks had shattered the peace of Israel.

What makes people go to such extremes? The question has become even more compelling in the wake of the Trade Center and Pentagon disasters. Americans have suddenly realized that what happened in New York on September 11, 2001, could happen on any other day and in almost any place. It's hard to defend against the violence done by someone willing to destroy himself. As Secretary of Defense Donald Rumsfeld said, "We cannot stop all the tactics of all the terrorists all the time."

A . **A motive rooted in human nature.** The reason for such behavior lies first of all in the fallenness of human nature. We are fundamentally evil. We don't want to believe that, but it is what Scripture teaches. Modern sociologists and psychologists have been trying for years to convince us that humanity is basically good. But that is not the case. Jeremiah 17:9 says,

"The heart is deceitful above all things, and desperately wicked; Who can know it?" "Man is born to trouble, as the sparks fly upward" (Job 5:7). God's own verdict on the human race is recorded in Genesis 8:21: "The imagination of man's heart is evil from his youth." And that was *after* all but one redeemed family of eight had been destroyed in a worldwide cataclysm because of the extreme wickedness of the human race.

In Romans 3:10–18 the apostle Paul draws a series of quotations from the Old Testament to describe humanity in these terms:

> "There is none righteous, no, not one; there is none who understands; there is none who seeks after God. They have all turned aside; they have together become unprofitable; there is none who does good, no, not one." "Their throat is an open tomb; With their tongues they have practiced deceit;" "The poison of asps is under their lips;" "Whose mouth is full of cursing and bitterness." "Their feet are swift to shed blood;" "Destruction and misery are in their ways;" "And the way of peace they have not known." "There is no fear of God before their eyes."

One needs only to look at human history to find ample evidence that this is true. History is a chronicle of bloodbaths and atrocities, and that is as true today as it has always been. All over the face of the earth and on every continent the shedding of blood by man's hand is common. We see this not only in individual acts of criminality, but also in corporate acts of villainy and in governmental acts of barbarity. Man is by nature a killer. We see it in the world wars of the twentieth century—the bloodiest century on record. We see it in the terrorist actions that are on the rise today. We see it in tribal societies, and we see it even in so-called civilized societies. It is evident everywhere, on the streets of our own cities and in the rugged wastelands of Afghanistan. Killing and violence are endemic to the whole human race.

The first crime recorded in the Bible was an act of violence. We read about it in Genesis 4. Cain murdered his own brother in a fit of jealousy, and that launched human history on its course of murder and mayhem.

Why does this happen? Scripture gives a plain, straightforward answer. James 4:1 raises the very question the whole world is currently asking: "Where do wars and fights come from among you?"

The answer is clear: "Do they not come from your desires for pleasure that war in your members?" "Members" includes both the physical and spiritual nature of the human being. James, writing under the inspiration of the Holy Spirit, suggests that it is the desire for pleasure inside us that generates war. The Greek word translated "wars" is *polemos*, and it refers to a prolonged state of conflict—warfare. The word translated "fights" is *mache*, which speaks of separate, individual battles. What causes wars and battles? Where do such conflicts arise?

It comes down to this: Evil desires for pleasure and self-fulfillment are what motivate people to wage war. James uses the Greek word *hedone*, which speaks of sensual delights—human lusts. That is the same Greek word from which we get "hedonism"—our name for a way of life devoted to the pursuit of sensual pleasures. (Hedonists live for the fulfillment of their own desires. They live to satisfy themselves, to get what they want, to take what fulfills them.) So the terminology James employs speaks of the yearning of self-love, the yearning to fulfill selfish pleasures. That is why people wage wars—because they want things, and someone else stands in the way.

Verse 2 further develops it: "You lust and do not have." That's the problem. You want some pleasure you don't have. It's a hedonistic compulsion, an internal drive, but it is thwarted. You want your pleasure, and you want it so badly that it produces conflict. The conflict begins inside the person. But someone else is in the way; so what had begun as an internal conflict becomes a murderous intention toward that other person. Ultimately, the person with the thwarted desire commits murder, which may lead to mayhem and even to war. That's the ultimate motive behind war. Notice that it is rooted in human nature.

In other words, people are not basically good; we're basically evil. If we did not have laws, law enforcement, and harsh penalties for murder, the whole of humanity would be killing itself all the time. People are driven by their own selfish desires. They are driven by their own need to fulfill their passions for what they feel will satisfy them. They are driven by a consuming hedonism. And anyone in the way may have to be sacrificed to fulfill that desire.

I recently read a book called *Neighbors*.[3] It's the story of the Polish town of Jedwabne during World War II. About sixteen hundred Poles and sixteen hundred Jews had lived there peacefully side by side for many generations. The town was under Soviet control at the outset of the war. But in June of 1941, Jedwabne came under German occupation. Within days, the Polish population of that town slaughtered virtually all their Jewish neighbors in a single day. Only seven Jews survived to tell the tale. There had been no racial strife in Jedwabne, and no anti-Jewish propaganda from Germany had reached that community. But within days of the German occupation, one half of that town viciously murdered the other half. Some were beheaded. Others were drowned. Still others were tortured to death, including mothers who were savagely beaten with their infants still in their arms. As dusk fell that evening, the remaining Jews were herded into a barn, which was doused with gasoline and set ablaze. The citizens of Jedwabne themselves committed the massacre; the Nazi army did not participate in the killings.

Why did those otherwise ordinary people slaughter their lifelong neighbors? Their families had lived peaceably together for more than three hundred years. They had worked together; they went to school together; they had patronized one another's businesses. But in a two-week period they went from being neighbors to being mass murderers. Why? Were they ordered to do it? No. Were they driven by latent anti-semitic passions? There is no evidence of that. All that happened was that the Germans took over the town and said, "You can kill them if you want and take their land and possessions." So they did it. Given free reign, their murderous lusts took over. That's powerful evidence of the wickedness of the human heart.

We see things like this on a smaller scale every day in the news. A few weeks before the recent terrorist attacks, a Russian young man in Sacramento went on a killing spree, systematically murdering members of his own family. Why? Because he thought they stood in the way of his fulfillment. There is no end to the horrors people are capable of in their quest for self-fulfillment. In 1994 Susan Smith deliberately drowned her own children in a South Carolina lake and claimed they had been kidnapped. Why? Her boyfriend had said he did not want to be responsible for raising another man's children. Those children therefore stood in the way of something she desired.

That is why people kill: They want something. Why did Hitler massacre the Jewish population of Europe? He thought they represented an obstacle to his Aryan supremacy. Why did Joseph Stalin massacre millions more? He thought they stood in the way of his world empire. It may be as vast as that, or it may be as simple as a person who kills a convenience-store worker for a handful of money. The desire to have something creates a conflict that ends in violence.

The apostle James goes on to say, "You murder and covet and cannot obtain. You fight and war" (James 4:2). And then he adds an amazing statement: "Yet you do not have because you do not ask. [Or] you ask and do not receive, because you ask amiss, that you may spend it on your pleasures" (vv. 2–3).

Here is an amazing truth: God stands ready to fulfill the legitimate desires of those who will seek Him. Psalm 37:4 says, "Delight yourself also in the LORD, and He shall give you the desires of your heart." But because of the perversity of the sinful heart, most people do not delight in God. They hate Him and reject Him. And therefore they simply do not seek to know and worship Him who alone could fulfill their lives.

Instead, they seek to find fulfillment in illegitimate ways. And in the absence of any restraint, the quest for selfish pleasure often ends in murder and violence. (In fact, there would be even more murder if it were not for the fear of punishment.) Whether the killing is done on a small scale or on a large scale, this is the ultimate reason behind virtually every act of murder: The wicked hearts of passionate people will not be denied their pleasure, so they desire to kill and sometimes actually do kill to get what they want. That is the pathology of the fallen human heart. That is why so many throughout history have been driven to extreme acts of murder. They are driven by passions that are so consuming as to border on madness.

So the first reason for these ruthless killings is found in fallen human nature. This motive has emerged clearly and has been widely discussed in some of the commentary featured in the media coverage of the recent terrorist events. Middle East experts, including some who share sympathies with the Islamic extremists, have suggested that the killers' intense hatred for America and Western society is stimulated by the fact that their own society suffers from extreme poverty and political disadvantage. Somehow in their twisted minds they have come to believe that the secret to their own prosperity lies in the downfall of Western culture, and they are determined to bring that about by any means possible.

฿,   **A motive rooted in biblical history.** There is also a historical reason for the recent acts of terror. The conflict that has given rise to the current tensions is as old as the Bible itself. Remember, the cultures of the modern Middle East are all ancient cultures, and the strife between peoples in the Middle East has its roots in the origin of nations as recorded in the Bible, as early as the Book of Genesis.

Genesis is the book of origins. "Genesis" means "beginnings." And in Genesis 10 and 11 we find what Bible scholars sometimes refer to as the table of nations. If you read the genealogies of Genesis 10–11, you will encounter a vast array of names. They are names of people and families who developed into tribes and nations. These genealogies record the development of early society as it developed from Noah. Of course, Scripture says that the Flood of Noah's time destroyed all humanity except for eight people—Noah, his wife, their three sons and wives. The descendants of those eight people who came off the ark ultimately repopulated the whole world. And

Genesis 10 begins the record of the generations that flowed from Noah through his three sons, Shem, Ham, and Japheth.

According to Scripture, Japheth, the eldest son, fathered what are now known as the Indo-European people. From Japheth came those who live in Europe and all the way across to India, including those in Russia and probably including even those who crossed the Bering Sea to populate North and South America.

Noah's son Ham, we learn, fathered families in Africa and the Far East, including the Asian world and some regions of the Middle East.

The best-known of Noah's sons was Shem. From him came the Semitic people of the Mesopotamian valley, the Middle East as we know it. Shem's offspring include the Jewish people and the Arabic people. Shem's progeny lived north, south, and east of the land of Israel.

That's a very simple and non-technical overview. The actual dispersion of races and nations is really quite complex, but that is a condensed summary of the biblical account.

The Middle East was the heart and the focus of the biblical account from the time of Creation. When God created Adam and Eve, he placed them in Eden. Scripture places that garden in the vicinity of the Euphrates valley, in the Mesopotamian region—the heart of the Middle East (Genesis 2:14). Of course, the Flood dramatically altered the earth's geography, but the Euphrates Valley remained the center of the biblical focus. It was the very place of Eden. It was there that the Tower of Babel was built. It was there where Nimrod built his kingdom (Genesis 10:9–10); and Nimrod is thought to be the father of the world's early religions. It was there that the city of Babylon was later built. It was there that Noah lived and preached before the Flood. It is a land rich in biblical and religious history. And today it lies in the center of the Arabic-Muslim world.

But four thousand years ago God made a covenant with Abraham. He gave a massive portion of that territory to Abraham and his Jewish descendants forever, "from the river of Egypt to the great river, the River Euphrates" (Genesis 15:18). That included everything from the Sinai peninsula and the Mediterranean coast through the depths of the Babylonian valley—the entire Mesopotamian region.

Abraham's father, Terah, was a worshiper of pagan gods (Joshua 24:2). History records that worship of the moon god was the most popular form of idolatry in the day of Abraham. Terah's name may even be derived from the name of the moon god. There were two great centers for worshiping the moon god. One was Ur, which was located in the Persian Gulf region in what is now Kuwait. The other was Haran, which was in the area of modern-day Iraq. Abraham was born in Ur and later lived in Haran.

So the land of the Middle East is rich with ancient history. It is the land where the Bible records that human history began. And according to Scripture, this same land will also be the center stage at the end of human history. The prophecies of Scripture tell us the world is going to come to an end in a great conflagration and a cataclysmic battle in the Valley of Megiddo, which is part of modern Israel. Massive armies from the north and south are going to converge in that valley from which the word "Armageddon" is derived (Revelation 16:16), and human history will culminate in an enormous battle where earthly kingdoms will be gathered together to wage war against Christ (Revelation 17:12–14). At that time, Scripture tells us, blood will be spilled across the entire land of Israel. At the end of it, Christ will return triumphantly, vanquish His enemies, and establish His own Kingdom in peace and righteousness across the face of the whole earth.

So the land of the Middle East is the most important piece of real estate in the world. None is more strategic.

Abraham, of course, fathered the Jewish people. In Genesis 12:1–3, God said to Abraham (then known as Abram), "Get out of your country, from your family and from your father's house, to a land that I will show you. I will make you a great nation; I will bless you and make your name great; and you shall be a blessing. I will bless those who bless you, and I will curse him who curses you; and in you all the families of the earth shall be blessed."

In Genesis 15:18–21, God defined the boundaries of the Promised Land: "On the same day the LORD made a covenant with Abram, saying, 'To your descendants I have given this land, from the river of Egypt to the great river, the River Euphrates; the Kenites, the Kenezzites, the Kadmonites, the Hittites, the Perizzites, the Rephaim, the Amorites, the Canaanites, the Girgashites, and the Jebusites.'"

In other words, by divine right from the mouth of God Himself, the region was given to Abraham and his seed. At the time of Abraham, all those tribes named in Genesis 15:19–21 were already occupying the land. Even though God promised the land to Abraham, it was already in the possession of those tribes. It was perhaps the most densely populated part of the world at that time.

By Abraham's time, some powerful nations had arisen. Mizraim (the Hebrew name for Egypt) had risen to prominence. In the region that later became Syria, several powerful city-states dominated. The entire Mesopotamian region was populated with large tribes and families and clans. All of them were idolatrous. They had abandoned the true and living God—the Creator God—and turned instead to pagan gods of their own making.

Therefore, when God promised Abraham that all the land would be his, Abraham and his offspring were set on a collision course toward religious and political conflict. The Middle East region is the richest land on the face of the earth. There are the coastal riches of the Sharon Valley in Israel; the fertile lands that go down the very spine of Israel; the vast mineral wealth of the Dead Sea; the immense oil treasures of the Arabian peninsula; the valuable timber that once covered Lebanon—all of this adds up to unequalled productivity and incredible wealth. God gave it all to Abraham and his offspring, the Jews.

But in order for the Promised Land to belong to Abraham's offspring, God Himself was going to have to open it up for them. And in the time of Joshua, God did finally bring the Israelites into the land as He had promised. He supernaturally delivered them from Egypt after four hundred years of slavery. He then miraculously protected and provided for them during forty years in the desert. Then finally He led them into the land that was to be theirs. Little by little, God began driving out the pagan inhabitants (Exodus 23:30). He fulfilled His promise to Abraham, not because of the righteousness of the Israelites, but because of the extreme wickedness of the nations that were driven out (Deuteronomy 9:5).

Some might question the justice of God's giving the land to Abraham in the first place. Was it right for the inhabitants of the land to be driven out and the territory to be given to Abraham? Certainly. Their expulsion from the land was a divine judgment because they had forsaken the true God and were worshiping the most loathsome kinds of idols. Their religions were based on human sacrifice and butchery. Some were followers of Molech, who supposedly demanded followers to sacrifice their own children by fire. They were people who gloried in wickedness and bloodshed. All of them had built gruesomely evil societies that glorified violence in a way that foreshadowed the savagery of the modern terrorists. They were fitting objects for God's judgment, because they reveled in every kind of abomination that He abhors (Deuteronomy 18:12).

Idolatry is judged harshly by God in every era. It was a just judgment for God to take away that precious land from those who turned their backs on Him. He gave it instead to a people whom He commanded to love and serve Him.

But because of their own disobedience to God, the Israelites faced a constant battle trying to posses what God had given them. The surrounding nations waged constant wars against Israel throughout Old Testament history. And because the Israelites persisted in their disobedience against God, they were ultimately taken captive into Babylon, and the land was made desolate (Ezekiel 33:24-29). They didn't lose their right to the land, because God had promised it to them forever. But they were expelled from the land they possessed, and from that day until now they have waged a constant struggle to regain their jurisdiction over it.

They will fully regain their land and possess it completely only when Christ returns in glory and turns their hearts to Him (Romans 11:11–27). Then, Christ says prophetically, "They will look on Me whom they pierced. Yes, they will mourn for Him as one mourns for his only son, and grieve for Him as one grieves for a firstborn" (Zechariah 12:10). They will embrace Him as their Messiah; they will come to salvation; and in that very day the Messiah Himself will give them their land.

In the meantime they continue to lay claim to that land, and as long as they do, they will face the enmity of the entire Arab world.

Disastrously, Abraham himself brought massive confusion into the promise of God by having an illegiti- mate son, Ishmael. God had promised Abraham a son and asked Abraham to trust Him. At the time, Abraham was about a hundred years old and Sarah was ninety, and they were barren. Abraham must have wondered how he could be the father of many nations if he couldn't even father a single child. One day his wife Sarah (then known as Sarai) came to him with a plan. She said, "See now, the LORD has restrained me from bearing children. Please, go in to my maid; perhaps I shall obtain children by her" (Genesis 16:2).

In other words, Sarah proposed that her personal handmaiden could be a sort of surrogate wife to Abraham, for the purpose of bearing him a child. And in an act of distrust toward God, Abraham followed his wife's suggestion. Hagar became pregnant and brought forth a son whose name was Ishmael. He was an illegitimate son; not the heir of God's promise; not the son of the covenant.

By now, however, Abraham had his heart set on Ishmael as his heir, and he pleaded with God, "Oh, that Ishmael might live before You" (Genesis 17:18).

God replied, "No, Sarah your wife shall bear you a son, and you shall call his name Isaac; I will establish My covenant with him for an everlasting covenant, and with his descendants after him" (v. 19). Isaac was to be the covenant child.

What of Ishmael? God told Abraham, "And as for Ishmael, I have heard you. Behold, I have blessed him, and will make him fruitful, and will multiply him exceedingly. He shall beget twelve princes, and I will make him a great nation. But My covenant I will establish with Isaac, whom Sarah shall bear to you at this set time next year" (vv. 20–21).

That is exactly what happened. Through Isaac came the Jewish people, but through Ishmael came twelve nomadic tribes that dwelt in northern Arabia (Genesis 25:13–16). Modern Arabs claim descent from Abraham through Ishmael. Some scholars would contest that claim, but no one can deny that the conflict between Jews and Arabic peoples over land in the Middle East has existed for millennia, since the time of Abraham. Scripture teaches that the conflict is rooted in the promise God made to Abraham.

Even today, the Middle East is filled with people whose ancestors have contested Israel's claim to the Promised Land for thousands of years. Two hundred fifty million Arabic people today surround five million Jews in Israel. The Israelis believe it is their divine right to have the land, but they won't be able to take full possession of it until their Messiah gives it to them.

In Genesis 16:12, the Angel of the Lord told Hagar, "[Ishmael] shall be a wild man; His hand shall be against every man, and every man's hand against him. And he shall dwell in the presence of all his brethren." In Israel today, untold numbers of Arabic terrorists, claiming descent from Ishmael, have declared war against the rest of the world—wild men in many ways, who have set themselves against every other culture, but dwelling among their ancient brethren, the Jewish people.

It was from this very environment that the culture of terrorism was born. All the terrorists and terrorist organizations connected with the September 11 atrocity are people who hate Israel and dispute the Jewish claim to the land of Israel.

So the historical reason for the terrorist action is clear: It stems from tensions rooted in biblical history, dating back to the time of Abraham.

C.   **A motive rooted in religion.** A third factor behind the terrorist action is related to the religious climate in the Middle East today. A radical strain of Islamic fundamentalism has unified some of the most violent factions in the Arabic world, and they are bent on destroying not only Israel but all of Western culture as well. They believe Western culture has weakened and defiled their religion.

There are some twenty-three countries in the Arab league. But their boundaries are being obliterated, and their national identities are being assimilated into one great force governed by Islamic fundamentalism.

In biblical times, the warring factions of people hostile to Israel were separated into small groups with limited power. That division helped keep the peace and ward off the threats to Israel's security.

Ever since God confused human language at Babel,

the diversity of human societies has helped keep evil in check worldwide. When all humanity was of one language and one mind, united against God, they were a formidable force for evil (Genesis 11:6). But after languages were confused at Babel, people scattered, and the result was a multiplicity of differing and competing nations. That diversity became an automatic check and balance in the distribution of world power. It helped prohibit any monolithic world evil.

In a similar way, the ancient Arab world was segregated into small tribes and fiefdoms for hundreds and hundreds of years. The diversity of so many factions kept any one group from achieving indomitable authority over the others. Nomadic lifestyles, deep-seated rivalries, religious differences, and the sheer number of separate groups kept the balance of power from tilting one way or the other.

But the Arab empire began to unite in the seventh century because of a man named Mohammed, who founded a new religion that became the rallying point of the Arab world. Mohammed was born in the city of Mecca on the Arabian peninsula in A.D. 570. His name in Arabic means "highly praised." He claimed to be a direct descendant of Ishmael.

At age forty, on a rugged mountain near Mecca, Mohammed began to see visions. He claimed the angel Gabriel had appeared to him. Through a series

of visions over several years' time, the angel supposedly dictated the text that would become the holy
book of Islam—the Koran. In 622, Mohammed fled an
assassination plot against him in Mecca and made his
home in Medina. That date marks the beginning of the
Islamic calendar.

Two years later, Mohammed began a holy war
against "infidels" (those who did not acknowledge him
as a prophet or Allah as the only god). By the time of
Mohammed's death in 632, Islam had become a powerful religious and political force. Within the first hundred
years after Mohammed, the Arab world was unified to a
remarkable degree, as that part of the world succumbed
to the power of Islam, mostly by the edge of the sword.

Muslims regard war as a legitimate means of turning people to their religion. A war whose purpose is to
bring infidels into submission under Islam is consid-
ered *jihad*, a holy war. Mohammed himself justified
and participated in killing and robbery against infidels
in the name of Allah. "Convert or die" has always been
the most persuasive tool in the Islamic "missionary's"
arsenal. And a penchant for death still dominates the
radical strains of Islam. Many fundamentalist
Muslims believe they are called to wage *jihad* against
infidels. They have also killed other Muslims who do
not embrace their fundamentalist fanaticism.

Islam has always conquered by the sword. And in

medieval times, Islamic armies converted virtually all of the Middle East by force. They also captured the land of Israel, and for the most part (though it changed hands several times during the Crusades, from the eleventh through the thirteenth centuries), they held control over it until May of 1948, when the State of Israel declared independence.

Throughout the Islamic world, there is a profound and deep-seated animosity toward Israel. That hatred is often transferred to the United States, because historically America has been the primary supporter and friend of Israel. In fact, in many ways, radical Islamists hate America *more* than they hate Israel. Their literature often refers to Israel as "the small Satan" and to America as "the great Satan."

There are approximately 1.2 billion Muslims in the world today. Not all of them hold the fanatical opinions of Islamic fundamentalists, of course. But nonetheless violence against infidels and the concept of *jihad* is fundamental to Islam and an inescapable part of Islamic history. Consequently, even many "moderate" Muslims have been loathe to make unequivocal criticisms of the terrorists and reluctant to support American efforts to end Islamic terrorism. The sacredness of *jihad* is too deeply ingrained in the Muslim belief system.

Islam is actually a word that means "surrender" or

"submission." Islam claims to be fully surrendered to the will of Allah. And the will of Allah, they believe, was revealed through his prophet Mohammed. The revelation is written down in the Muslim holy book, the Koran.

There are six basic articles of faith in Islam. A simple Islamic doctrinal statement would look something like this:

1. *Muslims believe that Allah alone is the one true deity.* He has neither mother nor father; similarly, he has no sons or daughters. He is not a Trinity; he is not the God of the Old Testament; and he is not the God of Christianity. Allah, according to Islam, is the god of all humanity.

2. *Muslims believe in all the "Messengers and Prophets of Allah."* According to Islamic literature, Allah sent thousands of prophets (Jesus being one), but Mohammed is the greatest of them all.

3. *Muslims believe in "the Revelations and the Koran."* They believe the Koran is the *most* holy book. Islam also recognizes other sacred writings, including the original manuscripts of the Bible. But Muslims claim that all other holy writings have been corrupted and tainted by translation and copyist errors. Only the Koran is pure, and every word of the Koran is the word of Allah, as given directly to Mohammed.

4. *Muslims believe in the angels of Allah.* They believe angels are created beings that have no material or physical needs. Angels require neither food nor drink. The angels are inferior to Allah but superior to humans, and they may be either good or evil.

5. *Muslims believe in a day of judgment.* All the dead will be raised to stand trial before Allah, and they will be judged according to their works. It is hoped by most Muslims that if a person follows Islam and does enough good deeds to outweigh the bad, Allah may allow such a person to enter paradise rather than sending that person to hell. But there are no guarantees of this. One's ultimate destiny is subject solely to the will of Allah. In Islam, there is no atonement for sin or promise of forgiveness, and no assurance of any kind, except for those who die in *jihad.* Those people, martyrs, are guaranteed eternal life in paradise.

6. *Muslims believe in "Qadaa and Qadar"*—Arabic words signifying Allah's timeless knowledge and power to execute his plans. Islamic determinism goes far beyond the biblical doctrine that God is ultimately sovereign over all, working all things together for good. Instead, Islamic predestinarianism amounts to a kind of fatalistic determinism,

where everything that occurs, both good and evil, is thought to come directly from the hand of Allah.

No Muslim can know for sure where he's going in the afterlife. Everyone's destiny is decided by Allah through an absolute, arbitrary kind of determinism. Most Muslims cling to the hope that good works might weigh heavily on Allah's scales of justice. But killing and being killed in *jihad* is the only sure pathway to heaven.

Muslims also have five duties, known as the pillars of Islam. Islam itself is said to be built on these five pillars:

1. *The first duty is the recitation of the Islamic declaration of faith, known as the* Shahadah. Most Muslims do this many times a day. The declaration is an Arabic chant that means, "There is no god but Allah and Mohammed is his prophet."

2. *The second duty is prayer five times a day.* These prayers (called *Salah*) are prescribed, formulaic rituals—written prayers that are memorized and recited by the faithful five times a day. Prayers are said at dawn, at noon, in the mid-afternoon, at sunset, and at nightfall. Islamic mosques usually feature a minaret, from which a person called the *muezzin* sings out the call to prayer. Prayers are always said facing Mecca, with worshipers kneeling in rows with no gaps between

individuals. Only in the main mosque in Mecca do worshipers kneel in a great circle, and there they surround a massive black stone cube, called the *Kaaba,* which is the focus of Muslim prayers worldwide.

3. *A third duty is charity* (known as *Zakat).* Muslims are required to give to the poor. To accomplish this, they are taxed 2.5 percent of their annual income and their property. "Charity" is defined broadly. In Islam, charity includes not only help for the poor, but also support for those engaged in the propagation of Islam. That is why some organizations well-known for supplying money to terrorists have been deemed "charities" in the Islamic world. By supporting *jihad,* they believe they are in effect supporting Islamic "missionary" work.

4. *A fourth duty is the annual fast*—actually a *month* of fasting—called Ramadan. Each year during Ramadan, faithful Muslims abstain from food, drink, and sexual relations during daylight hours. It is not a total fast, but an abstinence that lasts each day from sunup to sundown. Ramadan commemorates the first revelation that came to Mohammed in the year A.D. 610. Anyone who is sick, elderly, or traveling, as well as any woman who is pregnant or nursing, is

permitted to break the fast, but they have to make it up by fasting an equal number of days later in the year. If some physical inability keeps them from fasting, they must feed a needy person for every day of fasting they miss.

5. *A fifth duty, required of every Muslim at least once in his life* (unless it is utterly impossible by some restraint), *is a pilgrimage to Mecca,* called the *hajj.*

Those six articles of faith and those five duties summarize both the theology and the practice of Islam.

Islamic fundamentalists regard all non-Muslims, including Christians, to be infidels. Most moderate Muslims regard Jews and Christians ("people of the book") as somewhat better off than pagans and gross idolaters (followers of any other religion). But like all non-Muslims, Christians and Jews are deemed infidels nonetheless. A verse in the Koran (9:5), authorizes the faithful to "Slay the idolaters wherever you find them."

The faithful Muslim believes Allah himself is unknowable, distant, and impersonal. Moreover, Allah loves only faithful Muslims; he does not love sinners or infidels. Jesus Christ, Muslims are taught, was a mere man—a prophet, and not God incarnate. In their judgment, anyone who affirms the deity of Christ has made Him into a second god. Such a person is therefore guilty of polytheism and has become an infidel. This is an unforgivable sin (called *shirk*) in Islam, and it will send a person to hell forever.

That is the main reason it is hard for any Muslim to embrace Christianity. They have been programmed their entire lives to believe that Christianity is polytheism, and therefore, if a Muslim ever acknowledges Jesus as God, he will go to hell forever.

Further, Muslims deny that Jesus died on a cross, because they claim He was a prophet of Allah, and Allah would never let that happen to one of his prophets. Obviously, if Christ did not die on the cross, He did not have to rise from the dead; so Muslims deny the resurrection, too.

Islam further teaches that no one can have salvation but a Muslim. Even though a Muslim can never *know* whether he has salvation, only Muslims will have it in the end.

Clearly, Islam and Christianity are mutually exclusive. Both claim to be the only true way to God. Both cannot be right.

Again, Muslims die with no way of knowing where they are going. The faithful Muslim can only hope that Allah will judge him worthy of paradise. But there is no savior in Islam and no promise of salvation. Muslim theology has no atonement for sin and therefore no basis for forgiveness. Furthermore, Allah promises perfect justice, in which no sin will be overlooked, at the final judgment. It is therefore a hopeless religion with frightening prospects for eternity.

I'll never forget a conversation I once had with an Islamic man on an airplane. I asked him, "Do you sin?"

"Of course," he said. "I sin all the time. I'm on my way to do a sin right now." He explained that he had made plans to meet a woman with whom he was having an adulterous affair.

I asked, "What's going to happen to people who sin?"

"They could go to hell," he answered.

I asked him, "Why do you keep doing it?"

"I can't stop," he said.

"And," I asked, "how does your god feel about you?"

This is what he said: "I hope the god will forgive me." (He was translating *Allah* literally, for it means, *"the* god" with a definite article.) He repeated it wistfully: "I hope the god will forgive me."

I said, "Why would he do that?"

He shook his head sadly and said, "I don't know."

Remember, in Islam there is no atonement, no basis of forgiveness, no savior, and no assurance of eternal life. Christianity has the message of hope Islam lacks. There is a Savior. He has paid the price of sin. And He offers forgiveness and assurance of eternal life to all who will trust Him.

But Islam is a religion of hopelessness. It pretends

to regard the Bible as a holy writing, but denies every fundamental doctrine about sin and salvation taught in the Bible. In other words, Islam is based on lies. It is the product of "deceiving spirits and doctrines of demons" (1 Timothy 4:1).

Mohammed grew up in Mecca. He was a member of a tribe called the *Quarish*. His father, Abdallah, died soon after his birth, and his mother died when he was six years old. He spent his youth attending camel caravans and herding camels.

Religion in and around Mecca at the time of Mohammed's birth was idolatrous in the extreme. The religious center at Mecca housed more than three hundred sixty idols. These included tribal and household images worshiped by many different groups. One of the idols was a prominent black stone—the *Kaaba*. The Koran claims that the *Kaaba* was originally given to Abraham by the angel Gabriel, and that Abraham himself built the original shrine at Mecca.

So the society Mohammed grew up in and around at Mecca was an extremely idolatrous religious culture, and intermixed with the paganism were remnants of Old Testament ideas and beliefs.

That main idol at Mecca, the *Kaaba*, was a token of Allah, or *Al-ilah*. Dr. Robert Morey's research into the historical roots of Islam has led him to conclude that *Al-ilah* was the name of the moon god.[4] If true, it suggests that belief in Allah is rooted in the worship of the moon god—the very same god Abraham's immediate ancestors would have worshiped in Ur of the Chaldees. Indeed, Islamic holidays are coordinated with the phases of the moon, and Islamic symbols prominently feature a crescent moon.

Mohammed's role in Arab religion was to unify all worship in the name of one god—Allah, *the* deity. According to Islamic tradition, when Mohammed was a young boy, he was visited by the archangel Gabriel, who tore open Mohammed's chest, removed his heart, cleansed it, and put it back. This was supposedly the first visitation Mohammed had from angelic beings. The story of his life thereafter is filled with fantastic tales of terrifying angelic visitations and conversations with beings from the spirit world.

Could these have been demonic influences? It seems certain that they were. Mohammed interpreted them as angelic visitations—appearances of the archangel Gabriel—but they have features usually associated with demonic influence. They provoked intense fear in Mohammed himself and resulted in violent seizures. Mohammed would go into a trance-like, cataleptic state, during which he claimed he was under the control of spirits that communicated with him. Those periods during which he was possessed by spirits resulted in "revelations" that contradict the

Bible, undermine biblical morality, and tell fantastic mythical tales about the spirit world. They have all the characteristics of demonic possession.

Apparently, the powers of evil were working through Mohammed to invent one unifying religion that would put an end to polytheism in the Arab world and form the basis of a singular Arab passion that opposed both Judaism and Christianity. While giving lip service to the belief that the Bible is a holy book, Islam undermines and opposes biblical teaching at almost every fundamental point. If any religion qualifies as a "doctrine of demons," Islam does.

What Mohammed did under the influence of the powers of darkness was this: He took elements from several forms of idol worship and pieced them all together into a new religion called Islam. But in reality he made only one significant, monumental change. He made the new religion monotheistic, demanding that his followers recognize only one god, Allah, with Mohammed as his prophet.

Mohammed claimed the Koran was revealed to him when he was under the control of the spirits. He testified that he himself was not always certain whether the visions were divine or demonic. But his wife urged him to submit to the revelations, because she was convinced they were from Gabriel. So for twenty-two years, from A.D. 610 until his death in A.D. 632, he received revelations from the spirit that controlled him. These were collected, memorized and passed down orally at first. Soon they were compiled by his followers from memory, forming the Koran.

Mohammed built his whole system of religion on these demonic revelations, adapting and merging various forms and features from the idol worship that had always existed in Mecca. Again, his stress on monotheism was the novelty that ultimately unified Islam.

But it did not happen without a bloody *jihad* first. Remember that in A.D. 622, Mohammed fled Mecca for Medina and declared *jihad* against all who would not follow him. When he returned victorious to Mecca in A.D. 630, Mohammed destroyed all the idols in the shrine there, sparing only the *Kaaba*, the symbol of Allah. From that point on, Islam spread throughout the Arab world by the use of the sword. And within a short time, most of the Arab world was under the control of Islam and has remained so ever since.

Why would someone under satanic control destroy polytheism and institute a monotheistic system? The truth is that Satan is quite happy with monotheism, as long as the wrong god is the object of worship. Islam is nothing other than monotheistic heathenism.

Mohammed taught that the Jews had been rejected by Allah and cursed. The Christians, he said, were polytheists and infidels. He reinvented biblical events, making biblical characters into Islamic patriarchs. According to the Koran, for example, "Abraham was not a Jew nor yet a Christian; but he was true in faith, and bowed his will to Allah's (which is Islam), and he joined not gods with Allah" (3:67). Muslims also insist that Christ's disciples were Muslims, not Christians, because, after all, Jesus Himself was merely a prophet for Allah. Therefore, Mohammed insisted, Jesus must have taught the ways of Allah.

Mohammed furthermore declared it the duty of every Muslim to subjugate the whole world to Allah, if need be by holy war. For several hundred years Islam spread throughout the world by waging war against the infidel.

Modern Islam, until the rise of Islamic fundamentalism, has been less aggressive. Obviously, through the years and centuries many people who have followed Islam have *not* been as militant as the early Islamic armies. But Mohammed himself was an aggressive, deadly militant, who boasted of killing and robbery and other evil acts in the name of Allah.

So there is plenty of warrant in the Islamic belief system for justifying violence and *jihad* in the name of Allah. And the rise of Islamic fundamentalism is simply a return to the militant "missionary" efforts advocated by Mohammed himself. For people who want to perpetrate terror and violence against the non-Islamic world, there is plenty of justification for that in the fundamental teachings of their religion. Radical Muslims can find in the Koran and in Islamic history ample warrant for forcing people to convert to Islam by whatever means they want to use. They are convinced that those who will not convert are legitimate targets for almost any kind of violent *jihad*. After all, the Koran itself (9:5) says, "Kill those who join other gods with Allah wherever you shall find them; and seize them, besiege them, and lay wait for them with every kind of ambush: but if they shall convert, and observe prayer, and pay the obligatory alms, then let them go their way."

In the wake of the terrorist attacks against America, many Islamic leaders and media commentators have protested that Islam is a peaceful religion and that the Koran is opposed to violence. One commentator wrote, "Bin Laden's Islamic terrorists not only hijacked airplanes; they hijacked an entire religion."[5]

But it is not only Islamic fundamentalism and Islamic tradition that advocate *jihad* against all infidels. The Koran itself is filled with teachings that promote violence and advocate the spread of Islam by force. Consider these verses from the Koran:

"Allah is an enemy to infidels" (2:92). "Fight for the cause of Allah" (2:245). "Allah loves no infidel" (2:276). "Let not believers take infidels for their friends rather than believers: whoso shall do this has nothing to hope from Allah" (3:27). "Verily, the infidels are your undoubted enemies" (4:102). "O believers! Take not infidels for friends rather than believers. Would you furnish Allah with clear right to punish you" (4:143)? "O Believers! Take not the Jews or Christians as friends. They are but one another's friends. If any one of you takes them for his friends, he surely is one of them" (5:56)! "Fight then against them until strife be at an end, and the religion be all of it Allah's" (8:40). "Make war upon such of those to whom the Scriptures have been given as believe not in Allah, or in the last day, and who forbid not that which Allah and His Apostle have forbidden, and who profess not the profession of the truth" (9:29). "O Prophet! Contend against the infidels and the hypocrites, and be rigorous with them" (9:74). "Verily, of the faithful has Allah bought their persons and their substance, on condition of Paradise for them in return: on the path of Allah shall they fight, and slay, and be slain: a promise for this is pledged in the Law, and in the Evangel, and in the Koran; and who is more faithful to his engagement than Allah? Rejoice, therefore, in the contract that you contracted: for this shall be the great bliss" (9:111). "Believers! wage war against such of the infidels as are your neighbors, and let them find

you rigorous" (9:123). "Allah loves not the false,
the Infidel" (22:39).

The truth of the matter is that Islam today is the
most powerful system on earth for the destruction of
biblical truth and Christianity. Islam is the main per-
secutor of Christians all over the world. Thousands of
Christians are dying under Islamic persecution, especially in the Middle East, Africa, Indonesia, and other
parts of Asia.

As far as Islam is concerned, the world is divided
into two parts—*Dar al Salaam* ("house of peace"),
where Allah rules; and *Dar al Harb* ("house of war"),
where people are not in submission to Allah. It's either
peace, if you submit to Allah, or it's holy war, *jihad*.

In 1948, Israel, perceived by Muslims as an infidel
people, invaded the house of peace and turned it into
a house of war. That's why Yasser Arafat, the leader of
the Palestine Liberation Organization (PLO), and one
of the original modern Islamic terrorists, said, "Peace
for us means the destruction of Israel."[6]

The only condition of peace in the thinking of most
extreme Islamic leaders is the total and utter destruction of the nation of Israel. One Christian writer says,

When Israel won the first military conflicts with
the Arabs it was a tremendous defeat for Allah.

Finally, Ayatollah Khomeini in Iran explained that Israel is a judgment from Allah for the back-slidden condition of the Muslims.

The defeat of Israel, therefore, has become the primary sign of Allah's pleasure with the faithful Muslims. When Israel pulled out from Lebanon . . . it was heralded as the first Arab victory in more than fifty years of conflict. It was a confirmation that Allah finally is pleased with the violent path of the Iranian backed fanatical Muslim guerilla *Hezb'Allah* (meaning "Allah's Party").[7]

Many radical Islamic fundamentalists believe that in order to gain Allah's pleasure, they must defeat Israel. And that is why they have declared *jihad,* not only against Israel, but against America as well, because America is the superpower that is sympathetic with Israel.

War is a language Islamic radicals understand, and every war they wage is a holy one, a *jihad.* In Algeria over the past two years somewhere between sixty thousand and eighty thousand people have been killed because Islamists are waging war in order to turn Algeria into an Islamic state.[8] Islamic fundamentalists there have executed scores of women just for being unveiled, and they vow to kill more.

Throughout history, the violence of Islamic *jihad* has

been focused against Christians in many lands. From 1894 to 1918, Muslims in Turkey persecuted Armenians—killing several million—in what remains history's greatest atrocity against Christians. The current Islamic regime in the Sudan has been systematically committing genocide against Christians for more than a decade, killing as many as two million people.[9] Under most Islamic governments, conversion to Christianity is a crime punishable by death. And in some places, such as in Afghanistan, executions are carried out in public arenas, as if the beheading of infidels were a spectator sport.[10]

Islamic violence is certainly nothing new.

For eight hundred years Islam had unchallenged dominion in the Middle East, from the time of Mohammed on. The Crusades were an essentially futile attempt to regain Catholic control of the Holy Land by force. But Islamic control of the Arab peoples has never been seriously challenged. Near the end of the Crusade era, Islamic armies regained control of the Holy Land and maintained unilateral power in the Middle East until 1948, when Israel declared independence. The Arab world today is attempting to reassert its power and regain control of Israel, chiefly through terrorist efforts.

The agenda of Islamic fundamentalism is to conquer the land for Islam again, in order to rid the Middle East of an infidel nation. As earlier indicated,

Who Is Behind These Atrocities, and Why?

America has become a prime target for the terrorists, mainly because of our nation's support for Israel.

Meanwhile, Islam's power has greatly increased because Middle East oil has given the Arab nations an immense source of wealth. And much of that wealth has been used to fund the *jihad*.

The extremists are deadly serious. In a CNN interview, Osama bin Laden said,

> We declared *jihad* against the US government, because the US government is unjust, criminal and tyrannical. It has committed acts that are extremely unjust, hideous and criminal whether directly or through its support of the Israeli occupation.
>
> For this and other acts of aggression and injustice, we have declared *jihad* against the U.S., because in our religion it is our duty to make *jihad* so that god's word is the one exalted to the heights and so that we drive the Americans away from all Muslim countries.[11]

On February 22, 1998, bin Laden issued an edict calling for death to Americans, including civilians. At that time, he announced the creation of "The International Islamic Front for *Jihad* Against the Jews and Crusaders." He said,

For over seven years the United States has been occupying the lands of Islam in the holiest of places, the Arabian Peninsula, plundering its riches, dictating to its rulers, humiliating its people, terrorizing its neighbors, and turning its bases in the Peninsula into a spearhead through which to fight the neighboring Muslim peoples. . . .

We—with God's help—call on every Muslim who believes in God and wishes to be rewarded to comply with God's order to kill the Americans and plunder their money wherever and whenever they find it. We also call on Muslim ulema, leaders, youths, and soldiers to launch the raid on Satan's U.S. troops and the devil's supporters allying with them, and to displace those who are behind them so that they may learn a lesson.

The ruling to kill the Americans and their allies—civilians and military—is an individual duty for every Muslim who can do it in any country in which it is possible to do it, in order to liberate the al-Aqsa Mosque and the holy mosque [Mecca] from their grip, and in order for their armies to move out of all the lands of Islam, defeated and unable to threaten any Muslim.[12]

In a subsequent interview with *Time* magazine, bin Laden said, "Thousands of millions of Muslims are angry. . . . Hostility toward America is a religious duty, and we hope to be rewarded for it by God. . . . I am confident that Muslims will be able to end the legend of the so-called superpower that is America."[13]

This is the religious motive behind the terrorist attacks. Radical Muslims believe they have a mandate from Allah to wage *jihad* against Israel and America. They believe what they are doing is for a righteous cause. Their false religion has this sinister effect: Once the consciences of evil people have been freed to do evil, they will do it. Moreover, if they believe that by doing this evil they're serving Allah, *nothing* will dissuade them from doing it.

Returning to Muslim theology for a moment, remember that in the Islamic belief system, assurance of forgiveness is utterly lacking, and the hope of paradise is elusive. But there is one way a Muslim can be sure of heaven: die in a *jihad*. The Koran says, "And if you shall be slain or die on the path of Allah, then pardon from Allah and mercy is better than all your amassings; For if you die or be slain, verily unto Allah shall you be gathered" (3:151–52). "And they who have fled their country and quitted their homes and suffered in my cause, and have fought and fallen, I will blot out their sins from them, and I will bring them into gardens beneath which the streams do flow" (3:194).

The Koran further says,

I will cast terror into the hearts of those who disbelieve. Therefore strike off their heads and strike off every fingertip of them. This is because they acted adversely to Allah and His Apostle; and whoever acts adversely to Allah and His Apostle—then surely Allah is severe in requiting evil. This—taste it, and know that for the unbelievers is the chastisement of fire. O you who believe! when you meet those who disbelieve marching for war, then turn not your backs to them. And whoever shall turn his back to them on that day—unless he turn aside for the sake of fighting or withdraws to a company—then he, indeed, becomes deserving of Allah's wrath, and his abode is hell; and an evil destination shall it be. So you did not slay them, but it was Allah Who slew them, and you did not smite when you smote the enemy, but it was Allah Who smote, and that He might confer upon the believers a good gift from Himself; surely Allah is hearing, knowing this, and that Allah is the weakener of the struggle of the unbelievers. (8:12–18)

In other words, fight the infidel and you will go to heaven. Turn away, and you will go to hell. In all of Islamic theology, this is the only way a person can *know for sure* that heaven is his destiny: wage a holy war and give up your own life.

A motive rooted in sensuality. There's even something beyond the religious and historical motives for Islamic holy war. It is a motive rooted in the most wicked kind of sensuality.

How do you get men to kill themselves in acts of terrorism? How is it that so many Islamic men are persuaded to become suicide bombers, or to fly airplanes into buildings knowing that they too will die?

One thing is evident: There is no shortage of Islamic true believers who are willing to kill themselves in what they are convinced is an act of holy war. Palestinian suicide bombers first began to carry out attacks against Israel in 1994. By 2001, suicide bombings had become commonplace events.

There is a considerable amount of controversy about the practice among Islamic leaders. Suicide is deemed a sin in Islam, and many therefore believe every act of suicide is forbidden. Moderate Muslims have condemned the practice of suicide attacks as unholy, even in war.

But many leading Islamic clerics insist that such bombings are acts of *jihad*, not suicide. They say those who die in *jihad* are martyrs, even if they die by their own hands. In fact, some have argued that it is a noble act and a guarantee of heaven, just like any other kind of martyrdom. Sheikh Youssuf el-Kardawi, one of Egypt's most respected clerics, said, "The suicide mission is the loftiest form of *jihad*. We are talking about an heroic act of sacrifice and sanctification. The person who redeems his soul for Allah, sacrifices himself as a sacrifice for his religion and people, and fights the enemies of Allah."[14] The Palestinian Council of Religious Leaders issued a ruling saying, "These acts of sacrifice are legitimate, and their legitimacy is derived from the Koran and Islamic law."[15] Support in the Islamic world for suicide bombers has steadily increased. Recent polls suggest that as many as 80 percent of Palestinians say they support the suicide bombings.[16]

Radical Islamic groups, such as Hamas and Hezbollah, say they have no shortage of volunteers. Young men, sometimes starting as young as five years old, are trained for these missions. They are programmed and brainwashed for just one thing. And they are absolutely convinced that this is a heroic death and a certain entrance into eternal paradise.

One Palestinian psychologist said, "The amazing thing is not the occurrence of the suicide bombings, rather the *rarity* of them."[17] Indeed. If it is a guaranteed pathway to heaven, who can fault the "martyr"?

Muslims are taught to glorify martyrdom. Mohammed al-Durra, a 13-year-old Palestinian boy, was killed in a shootout in Israel. His mother said, "I am happy he has been martyred." She said she had given him a snack before he went to the shootout.[18]

One writer says,

> A recent review of the 140 official school textbooks of the Palestinian Authority, showed that all subjects are used to teach Palestinian children to admire the *shahid*, or martyr. The Grade 8 literature textbook is filled with songs and poems glorifying child death. "Draw your sword, death will call upon you, and your sword will go wild. Palestine, the young will redeem your land." In a grammar text, the following question is asked: "Mark the subject and object of the following sentence: '*Jihad* is the religious duty of every Muslim.'" Another: "Cherish the *jihad* fighters who quench the earth of Jerusalem with their blood." The Teacher's Guide directs teachers to drive home points such as "Jews welcome their own persecution because it is profitable," and "The Jews' evil behaviour causes anti-Semitic persecution, and they must be killed."[19]

The same article said this:

> Despite the strong prohibition in Islam against suicide, Hezbollah and Hamas recruit and indoctrinate youths for suicide bombings, playing on adolescent psychology. Typical recruits are 17 to 23, isolated boys, locked into adolescent struggles.

The boys are divided into small secretive groups where they collectively read Qur'anic verses such as: "Think not of those who are slain in God's way as dead. Nay, they live, finding their sustenance in the presence of their Lord." An almost mystical sense of togetherness is created, which undoes the adolescent isolation these boys feel. The same mechanisms that pull together a football team are used to create a terrorist group. Most of these boys are instructed to suppress their sexual urges, and not watch television, but promised unlimited sexual activity in heaven with virgins should they become martyrs. [Vamik Volkan, author of the book *Bloodlines*,] adds, "After the death of a suicide bomber, members of a terrorist group actually hold a celebration (despite the family members' genuine grief) and speak of a martyr's death as a 'wedding.'"

Most suicide terrorists are young men (a majority of them between eighteen and twenty-three). Most of them are single men. They are not necessarily from disadvantaged classes. Some of them are from wealthy families, college-educated men with apparently bright futures. What motivates such a person to kill himself in an act of terrorism?

First of all, if he is a true believer in Islam, he is seeking some way to be certain his destiny is paradise.

Muslims believe hell is real, and they obviously want to avoid it. By dying in a holy war, they have the best possible assurance, according to their belief system, that their destiny is heaven.

But there's something more that is so bizarre, it is hard for non-Muslims to fathom. Martyrs are promised that when they die they will not only go to heaven, but when they get there, they will be welcomed by seventy-two black-eyed virgins who will have eternal sexual relations with them.[20]

In other words, the suicide bombers, mostly single males with pent-up sexual desires, have been taught to imagine paradise as a perpetual orgy. And the shortest and surest way to get there, they believe, is death in an act of *jihad.* That is why so many are willing to commit suicide.

There is a strain of sensuality and evil desire that runs deep in Islam. The Koran (4:3) permits marriage of up to four wives. Mohammed himself had at least thirteen wives (some authorities say more). He married one of them, Aisha, when she was only six years old.[21] In addition, Mohammed kept many other concubines. He was clearly a lascivious man with a voracious appetite for sensual pleasure. And that is reflected in the Islamic concept of heaven.

The Koran (Surah 55) describes paradise as a lush green garden of sensual delights, where fair-skinned, black-eyed maidens recline on green pillows and luxurious carpets, eager to provide eternal and unbridled pleasure for the "faithful." In the impressionable minds of potential soldiers in the *jihad,* such a concept of paradise becomes a powerful erotic fantasy. Many have found it a sufficient motive for deliberately sacrificing their own lives for the cause of Allah.

Meanwhile, Islamic fundamentalist clerics and schoolteachers often reinforce the myth. A recent article in *USA Today* about the suicide bombers includes this vignette:

> At an Islamic school in Gaza City run by Hamas, 11-year-old Palestinian student Ahmed's small frame and boyish smile are deceiving. They mask a determination to kill at any cost. "I will make my body a bomb that will blast the flesh of Zionists, the sons of pigs and monkeys," Ahmed says. "I will tear their bodies into little pieces and cause them more pain than they will ever know."
>
> *"Allahu Akbar,"* his classmates shout in response: "God is great."
>
> "May the virgins give you pleasure," his teacher yells, referring to one of the rewards awaiting martyrs in paradise. Even the principal smiles and nods his approval.[22]

Children are actively recruited as young as age five to become willing martyrs. Sheik Hasan Yosef, a Hamas leader in the West Bank, told a reporter, "We like to grow them from kindergarten through college." A Palestinian television program for children—*The Children's Club*, modeled after *Sesame Street*—features the song, "When I wander into Jerusalem, I will become a suicide bomber."[23]

In Hamas-run kindergartens, signs on the walls read: "The children of the kindergarten are the *shaheeds* (holy martyrs) of tomorrow." The classroom signs at Al-Najah University in the West Bank and at Gaza's Islamic University say, "Israel has nuclear bombs, we have human bombs."[24]

Sheik Abd Al-Salam Skheidm, Chief Mufti of the Palestinian Authority police, described what suicide bombers who kill Jewish women and children in Israel can expect in the afterlife:

> From the moment his first drop of blood spills, he feels no pain and he is absolved of all his sins; he sees his seat in heaven; he is spared the tortures of the grave; he is spared the horrors of the Day of Judgment; he is married to 70 black-eyed women; he can vouch for 70 of his family members to enter paradise; he earns the crown of

glory, whose precious stone is worth all of this world.[25]

On May 25, 2001, *The Voice of Palestine Radio* broadcast a Friday sermon from the Al-Aqsa mosque on the Temple Mount in Jerusalem. In that message, the Palestinian Authority Mufti, Sheik Ikrima Sabri, said, "The Moslem loves death and martyrdom, just as you love life. There is a great difference between he who loves the afterlife and he who loves this world. The Moslem loves death [and seeks] martyrdom."[26]

But when one realizes that the heaven longed for by the martyrs is eternal sex in a sensual paradise, their love of the afterlife doesn't seem very noble. Nonetheless, it is one of the main lures that draw so many young, disenfranchised, single men into becoming suicide bombers.

Such a belief system is an extreme manifestation of the sin that has infected the whole human race. As a religious belief, it may masquerade as something devout and holy. But in reality it is a perverse and evil lie that invariably produces perverted and diabolical deeds. It is a graphic reminder that all religions are not fundamentally the same, as some would have us imagine. All false religion is a monstrous evil, and some of it has the potential of turning men into monsters.

For decades, Western society has lacked any sense

of moral clarity. Public opinion and public policy have been guided by a pervasive moral relativism, where nothing is deemed truly good, and very little is judged evil. Hence the lines have been systematically rubbed out between good and evil, morality and amorality, virtue and perversion, truth and lies. Post-modern Western culture has enthusiastically embraced this relativism, deliberately giving equal sanction to every belief system, every lifestyle, every political opinion, every set of values, and every moral code (or lack thereof). Our society has grown accustomed to rationalizing and tolerating the worst kinds of amoral behavior and wicked beliefs, and now it is even deemed politically incorrect to speak against many of the worst evils in our society.

But the events of September 11, 2001, make it impossible to maintain that kind of moral relativism. The terrorist attacks were unmixed and unmitigated evil by *any* measure. Thousands of civilians were indiscriminately killed for no reason other than to create destruction and terror. Both the act itself and the religious beliefs used to justify it are evil. Those who do not see these things as unmitigated evil have no business making moral judgments of any kind.

The terrorist attacks remind us that humanity is infected with evil and is susceptible to demonic lies. Unless the evil is plainly *identified* as evil and firmly *opposed,* it threatens to overwhelm and destroy us. Unless the lies are countermanded with the truth, society will continue to crumble.

Relativism is based on the notion that there is no objective standard of truth. If the relativists are right, we ultimately have no objective basis for facing the fact that the terrorists, their belief system, or their actions are evil. Of course, everything in the human conscience cries out that such things *are* evil. God has planted that knowledge in the human heart (Romans 2:15).

Beyond the shadowy subjectivity of human conscience, however, there *is* a clear and objective standard of truth: the Word of God—the Bible. Remember that the central values of Western society, including our most fundamental standards of justice and morality, are grounded in biblical truth. For millennia, the Bible has proven its power to expose evil, refute lies, and transform hearts for good.

The Bible is where we must turn in order to overcome the evil that threatens to destroy us. It is an *objective* standard of truth, something infinitely more sure and more reliable than mere individual opinion or human philosophy. It is the very Word of God, not the product of human speculation or demons (2 Peter 1:21). It is the *only* objective standard of divine truth that is worthy of our faith.

Three

The question we ought to ask is not why disasters sometimes happen. What we ought to ask is why disaster doesn't happen all *the time! This is the real marvel. It ought to amaze us that God, who owes us nothing but judgment for our sin, ordinarily chooses to bless us, bestow upon us His lovingkindness, and blanket us with His mercy. That ought to keep us in constant astonishment and wonder. And it ought to keep us on our faces before Him in gratitude.*

Three

Where Was God on September 11?

In the wake of the terrorist attacks, it seemed as if almost everyone began thinking and talking about God. The atrocity was of such monumental proportions that people naturally wondered what spiritual significance it had. Evil forces were obviously at work to cause the atrocity. Why did God permit it? Surely He could have stopped a few madmen bent on suicide from destroying thousands of innocent people. Why would He allow such a horrific thing to happen? For that matter, why does God permit evil at all? Is He angry with the human race? Or are the powers of evil so strong that even God has no power to thwart them?

Those are important questions that everyone must

face at one time or another. The terrorist attacks brought such queries to the forefront of public discussion like never before. Even people in the secular news media, who usually ignore spiritual issues or are openly hostile to religion, were asking those questions. In fact, two weeks after the disaster, I was asked to join a live panel discussion on CNN's *Larry King Weekend* to address those very questions.

The panel included representatives from a broad array of religious viewpoints. The group included a New Age mystic, a Jewish rabbi, and a Muslim theologian. Thus it was no surprise that the panelists did not agree among themselves on the answers. The rabbi, for example, said he believed God could not have prevented the terrorist attacks, because He has given "human beings the freedom to choose between being good people and being bad people." Another panelist seemed to agree that God Himself was victimized by the attack. The pantheistic New Age guru confused matters by suggesting that God is everything and everything is God; yet somehow the atrocity was the result of something else: "our ignorance about our inseparability with each other and our tribal instinct."

Unfortunately, not one of the panelists cited any authority for his answers other than his own personal opinion and subjective feelings. That is why when the question was finally put to me, I answered, "The Bible is the authoritative Word of God, and Scripture tells us that God is absolutely sovereign—that everything that occurs happens within the framework of His purpose."

Scripture says God "works all things according to the counsel of His will" (Ephesians 1:11). Indeed, if God were not sovereign over all things, how could we trust His promise that He will ultimately work "all things" together for good (Romans 8:28)?

John Piper has written,

> This "all things" includes the fall of sparrows (Matthew 10:29), the rolling of dice (Proverbs 16:33), the slaughter of his people (Psalm 44:11), the decisions of kings (Proverbs 21:1), the failing of sight (Exodus 4:11), the sickness of children (2 Samuel 12:15), the loss and gain of money (1 Samuel 2:7), the suffering of saints (1 Peter 4:19), the completion of travel plans (James 4:15), the persecution of Christians (Hebrews 12:4–7), the repentance of souls (2 Timothy 2:25), the gift of faith (Philippians 1:29), the pursuit of holiness (Philippians 3:12–13), the growth of believers (Hebrews 6:3), the giving of life and the taking in death (1 Samuel 2:6), and the crucifixion of his Son (Acts 4:27–28).[1]

God Himself says, "My counsel shall stand, and I

will do all My pleasure . . . Indeed I have spoken it; I will also bring it to pass. I have purposed it; I will also do it" (Isaiah 46:10–11). God is absolutely sovereign over all that happens, and nothing happens apart from His watchful eye or His perfect will.

I further told the Larry King audience: "That is not to say that God creates evil. The Bible says He does not, nor does He do evil, nor does he tempt anyone to do evil. But evil exists. It's everywhere. And God will ultimately overrule evil for His own purpose." Scripture promises that God will one day eliminate evil and evildoers from the universe forever.

In the meantime, we are not to think that evil thwarts His plan, catches Him off guard, or nullifies His absolute sovereignty in any way. "The Lord of hosts has sworn, saying, 'Surely, as I have thought, so it shall come to pass, and as I have purposed, so it shall stand'" (Isaiah 14:24).

In fact, God is able to *use* even the evil that men do to accomplish His purpose. And thus He remains in absolute control of all things, even when it appears from a human perspective that things have gone completely out of control. God is still in charge, and His will is being accomplished perfectly—even in the midst of calamity and chaos.

Amos 3:6 says, "If there is calamity in a city, will not the Lord have done it?" In other words, disaster does not occur—even atrocities that are caused by wicked people for ungodly purposes—unless the Lord has a purpose in it. We may not see immediately what His purpose is. But we can know with absolute certainty that His purposes are always good, and righteous, and for the ultimate benefit of His people and the honor of His holy Name.

We should not assume, moreover, that it always signifies divine judgment when disaster befalls a people. It is utter folly to imagine that we can immediately understand the full meaning of every act of God's providence, or to declare recklessly that a particular tragedy is divine retribution or proof of God's displeasure against the victims.

We see this clearly in the Old Testament account of Job. The series of tragedies that happened to him reflected *Satan's* animosity to him, not God's. Scripture says Job was "blameless and upright, and one who feared God and shunned evil" (Job 1:1,8). But Satan despised Job, claiming that Job served God only because God blessed him (vv. 9–11). So God gave Satan permission to afflict Job: "And the Lord said to Satan, 'Behold, all that he has is in your power; only do not lay a hand on his person'" (v. 12). God would illustrate through Job the perseverance of saving faith, and the futility of Satan's attempts to destroy the salvation of those who belong to God.

The evil that subsequently occurred to Job was all from Satan. And yet God was still sovereignly exercising complete control. He strictly drew the limits on what He would permit Satan to do. Later (Job 2:4–6), He removed part of that restriction, allowing Satan to afflict Job's person, but prohibiting him from taking Job's life. Even then, God remained in control, and Satan could do no more to Job than what God sovereignly allowed.

This was not a cruel game. God had a good purpose in allowing Satan to afflict Job. The experience was even good for Job in the ultimate sense. God used it to deepen Job's faith, to perfect his understanding of God, to enrich his appreciation of the divine majesty, to show him the insignificance of mundane things, to refine his character, and above all, to show the enduring steadfastness of genuine saving faith. Those were weighty and important lessons, infinitely more valuable to Job in the scope of eternity than all the earthly privileges and possessions Satan had taken from him. And in the end, God gave back to Job much more in the way of earthly blessings than Satan had ever taken away from him.

Job's counselors were convinced the calamities were irrefutable evidence of God's displeasure over some secret sin Job was harboring. They asked, "Who ever perished being innocent? Or where were the upright ever cut off" (4:7)? But the perspective of Job's counselors was short-sighted. Affliction is not always proof of divine displeasure, just as prosperity is not necessarily proof of God's blessing. God makes the sun rise on the good as well as the evil, and He sends rain on the just and the unjust alike (Matthew 5:45). Calamity and misfortune aren't always merely punishments for sin.

Nonetheless, it is true that calamity is a natural and inevitable *consequence* of sin. And that is the real reason this world is filled with tragedy and misfortune. We are all sinners who have rebelled against God and violated His law (Romans 3:23). And the wages of sin is death (Romans 6:23).

That is why disaster and death are universal in human experience. "It is appointed for men to die" (Hebrews 9:27). We don't *deserve* comfort and blessing and divine favor. We deserve death for our sin. Every one of us is a willing participant in evil, and calamity is the inevitable result.

So the question we ought to ask is not why disasters sometimes happen. What we *ought* to ask is why disaster doesn't happen all the time! This is the real marvel. It ought to amaze us that God, who owes us nothing but judgment for our sin, ordinarily chooses to bless us, bestow upon us His lovingkindness, and blanket us with His mercy. *That* ought to keep us in constant astonishment and wonder. And it ought to keep us on our faces before Him in gratitude.

It *is* an enormous tragedy that so many people died in the terrorist attacks. I don't want to minimize it or trivialize it in any way. But the truth is that nothing happened to them that wasn't going to happen anyway. They were all going to die. Death is an inevitable fact of life for which we must each be prepared.

Every day in America, thousands of people die. About fifty thousand Americans die each week. Tens of millions die each year worldwide. Sadly, death is inevitable. Eventually everyone will die. We are more comfortable when people die one by one. It makes the fact of death easier to ignore. Every now and then, hundreds will die at once in a plane crash, or thousands will perish in a flood, an earthquake, an epidemic, or some other kind of disaster. Fortunately, such disasters are rare. They are especially uncommon in more sophisticated societies like ours.

But everyone *does* die eventually. That is reality. We try not to think about it. We go on blissfully living our lives with little regard for the fact that thousands are dying each week. Yet death is all around us. When the final death toll is counted from the terrorist strikes, it will probably be about six thousand—about the same as the average number of people who die on any typical day in America. I cite that statistic not to trivialize the horrific scope of *this* disaster, but to put in perspective the enormous reality that death is the universal consequence of human sin. We cannot keep death at a distance, as much as we would like to. Death is a plague on the whole human race.

Of course, one element that adds to the tragedy of the recent disaster is that so many people died who were not expecting to die. Death came to them abruptly. But that happens every day, too. It could happen to any one of us at any time. We need to be prepared for the eventuality.

As sinners worthy of death, we have no guarantee of life and no right to insist that God should grant us long lives. Our times are in His hands (Psalm 31:15). Life itself is brief and fragile. We cannot count on life. *Death* we can count on!

This is a constant theme in Scripture. In Psalm 39:5, David wrote, "Indeed, You have made my days as handbreadths, and my age is as nothing before You; certainly every man at his best state is but vapor."

Psalm 90, identified in the superscription as a prayer of Moses, says,

You are God.
You turn man to destruction,
And say, "Return, O children of men."

For a thousand years in Your sight
Are like yesterday when it is past,
And like a watch in the night.
You carry them away like a flood;
They are like a sleep.
In the morning they are like grass which grows up:
In the morning it flourishes and grows up;
In the evening it is cut down and withers.

—PSALM 90:2–6

The prophet Isaiah underscored the brevity of life with these familiar words from Isaiah 40:6–7: "All flesh is grass, and all its loveliness is like the flower of the field. The grass withers, the flower fades, because the breath of the Lord blows upon it; surely the people are grass." Job 14:1–2 says, "Man who is born of woman is of few days and full of trouble. He comes forth like a flower and fades away; he flees like a shadow and does not continue."

James wrote, "You do not know what will happen tomorrow. For what is your life? It is even a vapor that appears for a little time and then vanishes away. Instead you ought to say, 'If the Lord wills, we shall live and do this or that'" (James 4:14–15).

God is sovereign over human life. And why not? He is the giver of life, and He has every right to establish its boundaries. "It is He who has made us, and not we ourselves; we are His people and the sheep of His pasture" (Psalm 100:3).

The appropriate question is not, "Why did God allow so many people to be killed?" The real question is why He allows any of us to live at all. God is amazingly merciful to this fallen, sinful race. He shields us to a very large degree from the awful effects of our sin. We live under constant mercy, and when the ugly effects of evil are clearly shown to us, we should not be shocked.

We have grown so accustomed to grace that we don't understand the full effects of our own sin. But every once in a while, God draws back the curtain and allows us to see what evil looks like in all its horror, so that we can appreciate His justice when He punishes sin. We must never be resentful or think God is the one at fault when the consequences of evil are manifest. After all, we have all been willing participants in the evil, and *that* is what causes calamity to occur. The fault lies with us, not with God. The fact of His absolute sovereignty does not change that.

The prophet Jeremiah also pointed out that God is utterly sovereign, and we are utterly sinful. In light of that, Jeremiah said, it is never appropriate for us to complain when divine providence brings calamity our way. He wrote, "Who is there who speaks and it comes to pass, unless the Lord has commanded it? Is it not from the mouth of the Most High that both good and ill go forth? Why should any living mortal, or any man, offer complaint in view of his sins?" (Lamentations 3:37–39, NASB).

The New Testament describes an occasion that has an eerie similarity to the collapse of the World Trade Center towers. Two awful catastrophes had resulted in tragic losses of life in Jerusalem during a time when Jesus was ministering there. One was a terrorist atrocity of sorts. Pilate, the Roman governor in Israel, had ordered his men to invade the Temple and slay some Galilean worshipers, people from the same part of the country from which Jesus came. The episode demonstrated Pilate's brutality in a shockingly graphic way. Scripture says he mingled their blood with their sacrifices. In the other incident, a tower in Siloam (near the Temple mount in Jerusalem) had accidentally collapsed, suddenly killing eighteen people.

Luke 13 describes how some people came and asked Jesus to explain the disasters. Surely, they believed, these tragedies must have spiritual significance. Perhaps those who died were uniquely deserving of divine judgment.

Jesus corrected that misconception:

> Do you suppose that these Galileans were worse
> sinners than all other Galileans, because they suf-

fered such things? I tell you, no; but unless you repent you will all likewise perish. Or those eighteen on whom the tower in Siloam fell and killed them, do you think that they were worse sinners than all other men who dwelt in Jerusalem? I tell you, no; but unless you repent you will all likewise perish. (Luke 13:2–5)

The question troubling people's minds was this: Those people who died in the Temple were religious. They were doing what the Old Testament told them to do. They were worshipers. Why would God allow idolatrous Roman soldiers to go in there and kill them in such a violent fashion, so that their own blood was mingled with their sacrifice? And why did God permit the tower to collapse and crush people who were merely going about the business of their everyday lives?

Some were wondering if the people who died were secretly worse sinners than anyone else. Jesus answered that concern bluntly, twice repeating the same thing: "I tell you, no; but unless you repent you will all likewise perish" (vv. 3, 5).

This, Jesus said, was the main lesson people should draw from the terrorist incident and the tower collapse: Everyone dies. When they die suddenly, it doesn't mean they were worse than anyone else. Neither the people who were murdered purposely in the Temple, nor the people who died accidentally under the collapse of that tower, were any *more* deserving of calamity than other people. They were not necessarily worse sinners than the rest of us. We *all* deserve nothing but calamity and destruction, and if we do not repent and turn to God for mercy, ultimate calamity—worse than any earthly horror—*will* be what we experience in eternity. We will perish in hell.

Jesus' warning had a particular application to the people of Jerusalem in His day. Their whole society was on the precipice of sudden destruction by Rome—in a massive catastrophe that actually occurred less than forty years later, in A.D. 70. The whole city and the Temple were utterly sacked and destroyed. The loss of life was enormous. By most estimates nearly eighty thousand Jewish people perished. It was one of the most crushing military defeats the world has ever seen. Christ's words were a loving appeal for those people to repent and embrace Him as their Messiah before it was too late. It was their only hope of eternal deliverance from the evil that was coming to take their lives.

His answer to their question has an application today as well. Everyone without exception is facing inevitable death. Those who do not repent and embrace Christ as Lord and Savior will perish eternally without hope. His words stand as both a stern warning and a compassionate appeal to every person.

Death could come as quickly and as unpredictably to every one of us as it came to those who were struck down in the Temple and those who were killed in Siloam by the falling tower. The recent terrorist attacks in America are a graphic reminder for us. "I tell you, no [those people weren't any worse sinners than the rest of us]; but unless you repent you will all likewise perish."

Of the people who died in the Pentagon, the people killed in the World Trade Center towers, and the people who perished in the airplanes that were hijacked, we know that some were believers in Jesus Christ, but others were not. Death came without warning to all of them. And those who perished without Christ perished without any hope. They were not necessarily worse sinners than anyone else. But Christ's warning is clear: *All* who do not repent will perish without hope.

Jesus Himself said that is the chief lesson to be drawn from calamities like this. They are reminders to us that we must prepare for death, which is inevitable and could come at any time. We are all sinners. Death and judgment are certain. We don't deserve anything *but* death and judgment. But as long as God graciously blesses us with the gift of life, we have the opportunity to repent and receive His full forgiveness.

Immediately after issuing those calls for repentance, Jesus went on to tell a parable:

A certain man had a fig tree planted in his vineyard, and he came seeking fruit on it and found none. Then he said to the keeper of his vineyard, "Look, for three years I have come seeking fruit on this fig tree and find none. Cut it down; why does it use up the ground?" But he answered and said to him, "Sir, let it alone this year also, until I dig around it and fertilize it. And if it bears fruit, well. But if not, after that you can cut it down." (Luke 13:6–9)

The parable makes the point vividly. We are all living on borrowed time. God could say at any time, "Cut it down." But in His grace, He waits. "Just give it a little more time to see if it bears the fruit of repentance." That is the heart of God. He calls us to repent of our sin and embrace the gift of His forgiveness. And for those who have spiritual ears to hear and hearts to respond, He offers full and free salvation in Christ, with the promise of eternal life forever in heaven.

At least two and a half million Americans will die this year. Eventually, *all* of us will die. It's time for people to take life and death more seriously. Enough of our games. Enough of our obsession with material things, nonstop entertainment, and this world's pleasures. Now is the time to contemplate life and death, heaven and hell, time and eternity with the utmost soberness and solemnity. There is nothing in life more important. We are living on borrowed time. It's time to repent and call on God to save us from sudden and eternal destruction.

In the church, it is time for preachers to stop the theatrics, the trivial entertainment, and the sermons about self-esteem and pop psychology. It is time to speak of life-and-death matters in biblical terms. We're called upon to rescue the perishing and care for the dying—and that is serious business. It's time for Christians to make their lives count as a witness for the gospel. It's time to be serious about eternal things. What else really matters?

Four

Scripture is clear in teaching that God still ordains government as the guardian of order and justice in society, and He still gives government the authority to punish evildoers, even by waging war, when necessary.

Four

A Biblical Perspective on War

In the wake of the terrorist attacks, our nation and the world is poised on the brink of a major war. Within hours of the collapse of the World Trade Center, the President of the United States began speaking of war, and the media immediately began to print the word "war" in bold headlines. It is the first war of the twenty-first century. The goal in this war is not to defeat an enemy nation, but to destroy the terrorists' ability to foment fear, and to put an end to terrorist activity as a weapon against freedom. It is a war that will likely involve a deadly, sustained armed conflict in which many lives may be lost.

It is not a war America sought or started. The war

began the moment the hijacked jets hit those buildings and killed thousands of people. That act was nothing less than a declaration of war. If our government does not respond with force, we will ultimately have no choice but to capitulate to the terrorists' demands, and that would spell the end of freedom in America.

Although American opinion is uncharacteristically unified on the war, there are also, as usual, some who have loudly voiced opposition. Radical pacifists have come out in force to condemn any kind of military response. Some have suggested that the terrorist attack was a criminal offense rather than an act of war, and therefore the perpetrators should be hunted down, arrested, and brought to justice through the American court system, rather than killed by military means.

What does the Bible say about war? Is there ever a just reason to wage war, or do Jesus' words about turning the other cheek (Matthew 5:39) apply to governments as well as individuals? Are these terrorist attacks justification for America to go to war, or should we seek nonviolent solutions? Is our nation's lethal response justifiable by biblical standards?

It may surprise some to learn that in the Bible, war itself is not portrayed as inherently wrong, immoral, or ungodly. There are times when God Himself authorizes and condones war as an instrument of justice.

A Biblical Perspective on War

We know, of course, that the sixth commandment says, "You shall not murder" (Exodus 20:13). Yet in Genesis 9:6, God Himself instituted capital punishment as a just penalty for murder. He told Noah, "Whoever sheds man's blood, by man his blood shall be shed." Numbers 35:33 says that if blood defiles the land, "no atonement can be made for the land, for the blood that is shed on it, except by the blood of him who shed it." In fact, in the Mosaic law there are at least thirty other immoral acts and crimes for which God Himself prescribed the death penalty.

Moreover, God expressly instituted government as the means by which that penalty should be carried out. So while individuals do not have the right to take a life in an act of murder or revenge, there is a place for just retribution. There are crimes, including murder, that *require* retaliation and retribution in the form of death, and it is the government's job to see that the penalty is carried out against those who have committed acts worthy of death.

Similarly, God has given human governments the right to fight wars for self-protection and as a means of justice. The Old Testament is full of incidents where God Himself authorized war and even ordered the Israelites to wage war. How were the Israelites to conquer the land? By war. By armed conflict. The Book of Joshua includes a long chronicle of how God used the armies of Israel to destroy the wicked Canaanites at His command.

The Israelites were never given free license to kill by their own will, but at times they had explicit directives from God to wage war. In 1 Samuel 15:3, for example, God commanded King Saul, "Now go and attack Amalek, and utterly destroy all that they have, and do not spare them." Some of the wars God directed Israel to wage were shocking in the amount of bloodshed and carnage that resulted. Such a judgment was commensurate with the extreme evil of those brutal and war-loving societies. Those relatively few instances were the only true "holy wars" in history.

But God also occasionally used war as a means of judging His own people, Israel—even employing pagan armies against them. He used the pagan Babylonians to judge the Israelites, and then He employed the armies of Persia to punish the Babylonians for their desecration of Jerusalem. In Jeremiah 51:20–24, God speaks prophetically to Cyrus of Persia:

> "You are My battle-ax and weapons of war: for with you I will break the nation in pieces; with you I will destroy kingdoms; with you I will break in pieces the horse and its rider; with you I will break in pieces the chariot and its rider; with you also I will break in pieces man and woman; with

you I will break in pieces old and young; with you I will break in pieces the young man and the maiden; with you also I will break in pieces the shepherd and his flock; with you I will break in pieces the farmer and his yoke of oxen; and with you I will break in pieces governors and rulers. And I will repay Babylon and all the inhabitants of Chaldea for all the evil they have done in Zion in your sight," says the Lord.

Ten times the phrase "with you I will . . . " underscores the fact that God Himself would employ the armies of Persia as the instrument by which He judged Babylon.

Of course, no one today is receiving any direct revelation from God telling them to wage war. God has spoken with finality in Scripture. He is no longer giving new verbal revelation (Hebrews 1:1–3). The Bible is His complete and perfectly sufficient revelation to us (Revelation 22:18–19). He does not guide monarchs and presidents today by giving them special directives to go to war.

And yet, Scripture is clear in teaching that God still ordains government as the guardian of order and justice in society, and He still gives government the authority to punish evildoers, even by waging war, when necessary.

Terrorism, Jihad, and the Bible

It is a common misconception that the New Testament has overturned and erased the moral code of the Old Testament. Many believe war and violence are *always* wrong in this era, and they are convinced that this is what Scripture teaches. Some Christian denominations even teach radical pacifism as a tenet, basing their beliefs in Jesus' words about turning the other cheek. They teach their members that it is inconsistent with Christian principles to be a soldier, to fight in a war, or to advocate warfare or violence for any cause.

However, that is not the teaching of the New Testament. In Luke, we read of an incident where some soldiers came to John the Baptist and asked, "And what shall we do?" If he were a pacifist, John might have said, "Get out of the military. It's wrong." Instead, he said, "Do not intimidate anyone or accuse falsely, and be content with your wages" (Luke 3:14). His answer gave an implicit affirmation to their profession as soldiers. Instead of urging them to give up soldiering, he told them to be noble, honest soldiers.

A similar lesson may be drawn from Acts 10, where we meet Cornelius. He was a Roman centurion—the leader of a hundred men in the Roman army. Cornelius was a formidable soldier with a position of impressive authority. And yet Scripture describes him as "a devout man and one who feared God with all his household, who gave alms generously to the people, and prayed to God always" (Acts 10:2). That is yet another implicit commendation of a man who was both a Roman soldier and a righteous man.

The teaching of Jesus is filled with similar implicit affirmations of soldiering and warfare. In Luke 14:31, Jesus asked, "What king, going to make war against another king, does not sit down first and consider whether he is able with ten thousand to meet him who comes against him with twenty thousand?" In Luke 22:36, He said, "He who has no sword, let him sell his garment and buy one." Later, when Peter drew his sword and attempted to defend Jesus against those who had come to arrest Him, Jesus rebuked Him, saying, "Put your sword in its place, for all who take the sword will perish by the sword" (Matthew 26:52), rebuking Peter for a personal act of violence, but acknowledging the Roman government's authority to execute capital punishment against those who employed violence against their authority. And in John 18:36, Jesus told Pilate, "My kingdom is not of this world. If My kingdom were of this world, *My servants would fight*" (emphasis added), thus acknowledging the right of an earthly government to wage warfare.

Notice also how frequently in the New Testament the soldier is employed as a symbol for what a Christian ought to be. In Ephesians 6, for example, we are urged to put on the whole armor of God (v. 11). The passage goes on to outline a full array of defensive and offensive gear—spiritual weaponry, symbolized by the instruments of warfare. Paul also urged Timothy to "endure hardship as a good soldier of Jesus Christ" (2 Timothy 2:3).

Surely Scripture would never use a dishonorable profession as a good example for Christians. Christians are never compared to thieves or prostitutes. But the soldier is a perfect analogy for the Christian, because we are engaged in spiritual warfare. And by comparing us to soldiers, Scripture elevates the nobility of the profession.

Romans 13 makes the point inescapable. There we read,

> Let every soul be subject to the governing authorities. For there is no authority except from God, and the authorities that exist are appointed by God. Therefore whoever resists the authority resists the ordinance of God, and those who resist will bring judgment on themselves. For rulers are not a terror to good works, but to evil. Do you want to be unafraid of the authority? Do what is good, and you will have praise from the same. For he is God's minister to you for good. But if you do evil, be afraid; for he does not bear

the sword in vain; for he is God's minister, an avenger to execute wrath on him who practices evil. (13:1–4)

In other words, government as an entity is ordained by God for a purpose. The primary duty of civil government is indicated here. It is not welfare. It is not the reallocation of wealth. It is not merely to maintain roads and oversee other public works. It is not to educate our children. The *primary* duty of civil government is law enforcement. It is to punish evildoers so they can't harm other people; and to deter would-be evildoers by firm and swift punishment for all.

The apostle Paul wasn't suggesting that all governments are inherently good. As a matter of fact, he most likely wrote this passage during the time when Nero was emperor. Nero was one of the most wicked men ever to sit on the throne of Rome. Nero abused his authority to persecute Christians in one of the earliest and most vicious examples of Roman persecution ever.

And yet, Paul says, the *institution* of government was ordained by God, and He remains sovereign over it. Even when evil rulers are in control,[1] as is often the case, there is no biblical warrant to rebel and break the law, unless the ruling powers command us to disobey a clear commandment of God (Acts 5:29). God has established government to rule by law. And the means by which government is authorized to enforce the law goes as far as, and includes, the use of deadly force: the sword.

Governors, policemen, soldiers, and duly constituted officials who represent the government's authority are authorized to use violence to protect law-abiding citizens and to apprehend criminals, bring them to justice, and judge them for their crimes. Capital punishment falls under this sanction. (The sword is an instrument of death; the apostle Paul is not employing hyperbole.) War also comes under this sanction in cases where the evildoer is another nation or a group of terrorists hiding behind a corrupt regime.

When government representatives function as God has ordained, "they are God's ministers" (Romans 13:6). Again, that doesn't mean that the government itself is necessarily righteous. But its efforts to maintain peace and pursue justice constitute a righteous cause. "For rulers are not a terror to good works, but to evil. Do you want to be unafraid of the authority? Do what is good, and you will have praise from the same" (v. 3). Government as God has ordained it seeks justice. And justice poses no threat whatsoever to those who do good by obeying the law.

"But if you do evil, be afraid; for he does not bear the sword in vain" (v. 4). Government is expressly authorized by God as "an avenger to execute wrath on him who practices evil." Indeed, government is *mandated* by God to punish evildoers, with violence and death when necessary.

When a foreign nation or a group of people like the terrorists attack America, they have struck a blow against an institution of God. And our government has a divine mandate to wield the sword to bring justice to those who are responsible, even if that entails waging war.

This has nothing in common with the Islamic notion of holy war. America is not by any stretch of the imagination a godly nation. Nor are we called to make the world Christian at the point of the sword. Legitimate Christianity has always evangelized through the proclamation of the gospel. And although history records some misguided individuals and movements who thought Christianity could be expanded through holy war, that is not what Romans 13 is talking about. Such a war has no warrant anywhere in Scripture, and it is not what any serious Christian seeks.

The divinely bestowed authority to wield the sword applies to government itself, and not to any particular nation. Those who attack that institution ought to "be afraid," because a duly constituted government is authorized by God to retaliate, as "an avenger to execute wrath on him who practices evil" (Romans 13:4).

In other words, God has delegated a degree of temporal vengeance to the government. The government has the rightful power to kill. Again, it is the government's *duty* to seek vengeance against those who do evil and destroy peace.

I am convinced God gave this power to governments because of His mercy. Otherwise, evil people would dominate. That is why a just war is an expression of divine righteousness. To turn away from justice in the name of peace is not an act of love; it is a refusal to love one's neighbor as oneself. To dispense with justice would never bring any kind of peace anyway. It would simply allow lawless people to dominate the world in a deadly fashion.

That's why Hitler, who was systematically murdering millions, had to be stopped by a war in the twentieth century. That's why Saddam Hussein should have been eliminated from power before the Persian Gulf War ended in 1991. And that is why Osama bin Laden and the terrorist networks, such as those he controls, must be destroyed to stop them from killing more people.

Not every war is justifiable, of course. There are two kinds of war. One is *the war of evil aggression,* driven by human lust (James 4:2). That kind of war, rooted in wretched lust and evil desire, is the kind of war being waged by the terrorists. It is by no stretch of the imagination a holy war.

A Biblical Perspective on War

But another kind of war—the kind of war the American government is now engaged in—is *the war of just protection.* An evil aggressor has shattered the peace in a murderous manner, making it necessary to wage war to restore peace and security. Such a war has a defensive aim. It is protective. It is the last resort when all avenues of peace are exhausted. Waging that kind of war is a legitimate function of government. Remember, every government has a *duty* to protect its people. That is why war in this case is necessary. If the American government doesn't do something immediately, terrorists will continue their attacks, and many more people will die. There will never be peace. (God Himself is a warrior, because He is a God of peace.) This war is necessary to end the reign of terror.

In Habakkuk 2, God condemns wars of aggression. He pronounces woe against nations that plunder and loot and revel in causing panic and terror. "Woe to him who builds a town with bloodshed, who establishes a city by iniquity" (v. 12)! God gives no sanction to those who wage war for the sheer delight of violence. In Psalm 68:30 He speaks of scattering "the peoples who delight in war."

In the history of warfare it is not always clear who is the evil aggressor and who is the just protector. But in the current conflict between America and the Islamic terrorists, the lines are drawn quite clearly. The terrorists are evil men, with an evil belief system, intent on causing death and destruction to all who do not share their corrupted passions. They broke the peace by committing murderous acts of terrorism. They are the aggressors, and it is clear that they are evil. They must be stopped, even though a war is necessary to stop them.

Our government, in this case, backed by other nations who are our allies in this war, is the just protector. There's no lack of moral clarity in the way these lines are drawn. Our government ought to move forward boldly in the execution of the war, and we who are Christians ought to pray that our armed forces will be used both as God's instrument of judgment on those who have murdered innocent people, and as the power to restore peace.

As Christians living in America, we also need to devote ourselves anew to spreading the gospel and seeking justice and righteousness in our own nation. Again, America is certainly not *God's* nation. No one should think that everything America stands for is righteous. We are not exempt from the threat of divine judgment ourselves.

In fact, some have suggested that the recent atrocities are a sign that God is preparing to judge America. Are the terrorist attacks a harbinger of divine retribution for our nation's sins, such as secularism, lasciviousness, materialism, and abortion? Could all of this be a prelude to some type of cataclysmic judgment on our nation? Could the devastation in New York and Washington portend some greater catastrophe, such as chemical or biological warfare, that could bring our nation to its knees?

The answer to those questions are known only by God. We simply cannot discern all the purposes of Providence. No one can say with certainty what God has in mind for our nation until God Himself reveals His purpose. He gives no account to us of His actions. He doesn't need to. And we can claim no right to call Him to account. He is the Sovereign of the universe. He answers to no one for what He does. He does not owe us any explanation, even when His providential purpose includes calamity and war. He simply assures us that He is blameless, perfectly righteous, and altogether holy. And He bids us trust Him.

We need to heed the prophet Isaiah's message to the people of Judah when that nation was poised on the brink of divine judgment. They had experienced a barrage of humiliations—trouble and defeat everywhere, even at the hands of idolatrous armies. Their enemies had plundered the treasures of the Hebrew nation, taken her people captive, and destroyed her national glory. Worse, God, through the prophet Isaiah, was telling them that things were only going to get worse. It was just a matter of time before Jerusalem would be conquered and the Temple itself laid waste. The people who weren't killed would be taken to Babylon as captives.

It was a hard judgment to swallow because the Israelites were the people of God's promise. They were the children of Abraham, Isaac, and Jacob. They were the covenant nation. Yet God was doing nothing to protect them. Through His prophets He was even foretelling their defeat. And their hearts cried out to know why.

Of course, the reason was that they had pursued a course of sin for many generations. They had turned their backs on God. They themselves were guilty of idolatry. But by comparing themselves with the more extreme wickedness of other nations, they felt they were undeserving of divine judgment. And so they begged for an explanation.

The Lord reminded them that He owed them no answers. In Isaiah 45:5–10, we read this:

> I am the LORD, and there is no other; there is no
> God besides Me. I will gird you, though you have
> not known Me, that they may know from the ris-
> ing of the sun to its setting that there is none
> besides Me. I am the LORD, and there is no other;
> I form the light and create darkness, I make
> peace and create calamity; I, the Lord, do all
> these things.' Rain down, you heavens, from

above, and let the skies pour down righteousness; let the earth open, let them bring forth salvation, and let righteousness spring up together. I, the LORD, have created it. Woe to him who strives with his Maker! Let the potsherd strive with the potsherds of the earth! Shall the clay say to him who forms it, 'What are you making?' Or shall your handiwork say, 'He has no hands'? Woe to him who says to his father, 'What are you begetting?' Or to the woman, 'What have you brought forth?'"

The potter doesn't have to answer to the clay. Parents are not accountable to their own infants. Likewise, God is not accountable to His creatures. The very attitude that challenges God is borne out of sin and rebellion.

All of this affirms that God is God. He is the Creator. He is sovereign. He is in control. He does exactly what He wants to do. And we have absolutely no right to interrogate Him. It all culminates with the prophet's exclamation in Isaiah 45:15: "Truly You are God, who hide Yourself, O God of Israel, the Savior!" This was not a complaint. It was praise. It was an expression of adoration. It was a statement of worship, and the exclamation point at the end is fitting.

What Isaiah meant was this: God is in control of

everything, including calamity. He is working His own purpose even through the evil that befell His people at the hands of a more wicked nation. We can't always see clearly what He is doing or why. We can't always discern His specific purpose in an event or a series of events. Nonetheless, He is there in the calamity just as surely as He is there in the blessing. And He has a *good* purpose in it, even when we can't see what that purpose is.

I love how verse 15 ends: "O God of Israel, the Savior!" In essence, Isaiah was saying, "I can't see and I can't know all the reasons for what You're doing; but this I know: You are a Savior!"

Isaiah realized that ultimately, although we cannot fathom all the mysteries of divine providence, and we know God has every right to judge sinful individuals and nations, we *also* know that He is a Savior. And His central objective in all His dealings with humanity is the salvation of sinners. Thus Isaiah looked beyond the immediate threat of judgment and expressed faith that the end of God's purpose was redemptive: "Israel shall be saved by the Lord with an everlasting salvation" (v. 17).

In verses 18–21, the Lord speaks again:

> For thus says the Lord, who created the heavens,
> who is God, who formed the earth and made it,
> who has established it, who did not create it in

vain, who formed it to be inhabited: "I am the Lord, and there is no other. I have not spoken in secret, in a dark place of the earth; I did not say to the seed of Jacob, 'Seek Me in vain'; I, the Lord, speak righteousness, I declare things that are right. Assemble yourselves and come; draw near together, you who have escaped from the nations. They have no knowledge, who carry the wood of their carved image, and pray to a god that cannot save. Tell and bring forth your case; yes, let them take counsel together. Who has declared this from ancient time? Who has told it from that time? Have not I, the Lord? And there is no other God besides Me, *a just God and a Savior;* there is none besides Me" (emphasis added).

That is followed by an invitation. It is an invitation that still applies to America in the twenty-first century. It is an invitation that applies to each individual: "Look to Me, and be saved, all you ends of the earth! For I am God, and there is no other" (v. 22).

War was declared by the terrorists who hijacked those planes and used them as weapons of mass destruction. The catastrophe has awakened us to the fragile nature of life. It has jolted us with the reality of imminent war. It has made us aware of an insecure future. It has brought us face to face with the horrors of evil. It has confronted us with the awful reality of sin, from which none of us is exempt. Above all, it has turned our hearts to spiritual matters and reminded us that we need to be prepared for the one certainty we all face: death.

In a sermon preached by Charles Spurgeon, the famous English Baptist pastor, in 1861, days after two separate railway accidents near London had taken thirty-eight lives, he said,

> Let us remember that death will come to us as it did to them, with *terrors*. Not with the crash of broken timbers, perhaps, not with the darkness of the tunnel, not with the smoke and with the steam, not with the shrieks of women and the groans of dying men, but yet with terrors. For meet death where we may, if we be not in Christ, and if the shepherd's rod and staff do not comfort us, to die must be an awful and tremendous thing. Yes, in thy body, O sinner, with downy pillows beneath thy head, and a wife's tender arm to bear thee up, and a tender hand to wipe thy clammy sweat, thou will find it awful work to face the monster and feel his sting, and enter into his dread dominion. It is awful work at any time, and at every time, under the best and most propitious circumstances, for a man to die unprepared.

In prosperous times people tend to look at eternal matters superficially. They are consumed with what is physical and what is fashionable. They build their lives on the fragile foundation of earthly values, and they fix their concerns on temporal things. Then when disaster hits, they are shattered by sadness, panic, and fear. Reality invades their world and dashes their dreams to pieces. This is a great opportunity for the gospel. Before September 11, people were living comfortably, in a state of indifference to the supernatural powers at work in the world. But now our whole nation is alert to the reality of sin and death and hell.

God is hidden in everything that has occurred, and He is working His sovereign purpose. We don't know all His plans for the future, but we do know this: He is the Savior. And He's calling people to salvation.

Five

Scripture calls the Savior "the Lord Jesus Christ, our hope" (1 Timothy 1:1). He is the embodiment of all true hope.

Five

Is There Hope?

THE EVENTS OF SEPTEMBER 11, 2001 left multitudes feeling fearful, confused, and shaken. People who just days before the incident were blithely unconcerned about the future are now struggling with an intense sense of hopelessness.

The Bible offers the only hope that really matters. It is the kind of hope Islam cannot offer. Neither can materialism, secularism, humanism, or any of the other popular religions and philosophies that have gained dominance in Western society over the past half century. It is the hope of eternal life. "This is the testimony: that God has given us eternal life, and this life is in His Son" (1 John 5:11). Christ is the *only* way of life. "Nor is there salvation in any other, for there is no other name under heaven given among men by which we must be saved" (Acts 4:12). But those who embrace Him by faith find in Him full salvation and the assurance of heaven eternally. "As many as received Him, to them He gave the right to become children of God, to those who believe in His name" (John 1:12).

That is why Scripture calls the Savior "the Lord Jesus Christ, our hope" (1 Timothy 1:1). He is the embodiment of all true hope.

To those reading this book who do not know Jesus Christ as Savior and Lord, I urge you to consider these truths with an open heart:

1. *You cannot please God through your own efforts or your own intelligence.*

> The carnal mind is enmity against God; for it is not subject to the law of God, nor indeed can be. So then, those who are in the flesh cannot please God. (Romans 8:7–8)

> Can the Ethiopian change his skin or the leopard its spots? Then may you also do good who are accustomed to do evil. (Jeremiah 13:23)

> But the natural man does not receive the things

of the Spirit of God, for they are foolishness to him; nor can he know them, because they are spiritually discerned. (1 Corinthians 2:14)

2. *If you continue in unbelief and sin, there is nothing in your ultimate future but death followed by God's wrath.*

> It is appointed for men to die once, but after this the judgment. (Hebrews 9:27)

> There is none righteous, no, not one . . . . for all have sinned and fall short of the glory of God. (Romans 3:10, 23)

> Do you not know that the unrighteous will not inherit the kingdom of God? Do not be deceived. Neither fornicators, nor idolaters, nor adulterers, nor homosexuals, nor sodomites, nor thieves, nor covetous, nor drunkards, nor revilers, nor extortioners will inherit the kingdom of God. (1 Corinthians 6:9–10)

> Remember, Jesus said, "I tell you, no; but unless you repent you will all likewise perish." (Luke 13:3, 5)

3. *Nevertheless, God offers salvation freely to all who turn to Christ in faith.*

Believe on the Lord Jesus Christ, and you will be saved. (Acts 16:31)

Whoever calls on the name of the LORD shall be saved. (Romans 10:13)

He is also able to save to the uttermost those who come to God through Him. (Hebrews 7:25)

Christ said, "I am the Alpha and the Omega, the Beginning and the End. I will give of the fountain of the water of life freely to him who thirsts." (Revelation 21:6)

Let him who thirsts come. Whoever desires, let him take the water of life freely. (Revelation 22:17)

Ho! Everyone who thirsts, come to the waters; and you who have no money, come, buy and eat. Yes, come, buy wine and milk without money and without price. Why do you spend money for what is not bread, and your wages for what does not satisfy? Listen carefully to Me, and eat what is good, and let your soul delight itself in abundance. . . . Seek the Lord while He may be found, call upon Him while He is near. Let the wicked forsake his way, and the unrighteous man his thoughts; let him return to the Lord, and He will have mercy on him; and to our God, for He will abundantly pardon. (Isaiah 55:1–3, 6–7)

4. *Salvation was purchased by Jesus Christ, who bore the full penalty of sin on behalf of all who would ever trust Him.*

Surely He has borne our griefs and carried our sorrows; Yet we esteemed Him stricken, smitten by God, and afflicted. But He was wounded for our transgressions, He was bruised for our iniquities; the chastisement for our peace was upon Him, and by His stripes we are healed. All we like sheep have gone astray; we have turned, every one, to his own way; and the Lord has laid on Him the iniquity of us all. (Isaiah 53:4–6)

For Christ also suffered once for sins, the just for the unjust, that He might bring us to God, being put to death in the flesh but made alive by the Spirit. (1 Peter 3:18)

Christ died for our sins according to the Scriptures. (1 Corinthians 15:3)

5. *He rose from the dead, thus signifying that salvation is fully accomplished.*

He was buried, and . . . He rose again the third day according to the Scriptures. (1 Corinthians 15:4)

God raised [Him] up, having loosed the pains of death, because it was not possible that He should be held by it. (Acts 2:24)

He has appointed a day on which He will judge the world in righteousness by the Man whom He has ordained. He has given assurance of this to all by raising Him from the dead. (Acts 17:31)

Jesus Christ our Lord . . . was born of the seed of David according to the flesh, and declared to be the Son of God with power according to the Spirit of holiness, by the resurrection from the dead. (Romans 1:3-4)

6. *Salvation is offered freely to all who believe.*

Let him who thirsts come. Whoever desires, let him take the water of life freely. (Revelation 22:17)

Jesus said, "Come to Me, all you who labor and are heavy laden, and I will give you rest. Take My yoke upon you and learn from Me, for I am gentle and lowly in heart, and you will find rest for your souls. For My yoke is easy and My burden is light." (Matthew 11:28–30)

For God so loved the world that He gave His only begotten Son, that whoever believes in Him should not perish but have everlasting life. (John 3:16)

He who believes in Him is not condemned; but he who does not believe is condemned already, because he has not believed in the name of the only begotten Son of God (John 3:18)

Most assuredly, I say to you, he who hears My word and believes in Him who sent Me has ever-lasting life, and shall not come into judgment, but has passed from death into life. (John 5:24)

If you confess with your mouth the Lord Jesus and believe in your heart that God has raised Him from the dead, you will be saved. (Romans 10:9)

7. *Salvation is possible only because Christ's perfect righteousness is imputed to all who believe.* This righteousness cannot be earned by any religious works or meritorious efforts. It can be ours only because God graciously imputes it to us by faith.

To him who does not work but believes on Him who justifies the ungodly, his faith is accounted for righteousness. . . . God imputes righteousness apart from works: blessed are those whose lawless deeds are forgiven, And whose sins are covered; blessed is the man to whom the Lord shall not impute sin. (Romans 4:5–8)

[We are] justified freely by His grace through the redemption that is in Christ Jesus. (Romans 3:24)

8. *Only this imputed righteousness of Christ is good enough to make us acceptable to God.*

Even the apostle Paul said he did not want to stand before God with a righteousness of his own. This great apostle knew that, despite his own faithfulness, despite all the accumulation of good works in his life, the only hope he had for being justified before God was a perfect righteousness imputed to him from a source outside himself. He found that justifying righteousness in the perfect righteousness of Christ, which is imputed by faith to believers. Therefore, he said his great, driving desire was to "be found in [Christ], not having my own righteousness, which is from the law, but that which is through faith in Christ, the righteousness which is from God by faith" (Philippians 3:9).

The eternal life Christ grants believers is certain and sure: "This is the testimony: that God has given us eternal life, and this life is in His Son. He who has the Son has life; he who does not have the Son of God does not have life. These things I have written to you who believe in the name of the Son of God, that you may know that you have eternal life, and that you may continue to believe in the name of the Son of God" (1 John 5:11–13).

My prayer for you is that you will trust Christ alone for the righteousness that can make you acceptable to God. Don't make the mistake of those who, "being ignorant of God's righteousness, and seeking to establish their own righteousness, have not submitted to the righteousness of God" (Romans 10:3).

When you have trusted Jesus Christ alone as your only Savior from sin and hell, you will have hope. His promise of eternal life is as good as His Word, and there is no better foundation for hope than that.

Consider the following promise: "Therefore, having been justified by faith, we have peace with God through our Lord Jesus Christ, through whom also we have access by faith into this grace in which we stand, and rejoice in hope of the glory of God" (Romans 5:1–2).

For more information about what it means
to follow Christ, please contact
Grace to You
PO Box 4000
Panorama City, CA 91412

Endnotes

Chapter One

1. The bloodiest battle of the Civil War was Antietam, where more than 23,000 men were reported injured or missing. The actual death toll from that battle is unknown, but conservative estimates set the figure at around 5,000. (Rick Hampson, "Minute by minute, fear envelops the country," *USA Today*, September 13, 2001).

Chapter Two

1. *Taliban* means "students of religion."
2. Karen Matusic, "Bin Laden Warned of 'Unprecedented' Attack" Reuters, September 13, 2001.
3. Jan T. Gross, *Neighbors: The Destruction of the Jewish Community in Jedwabne, Poland* (Princeton, N. J.: Princeton University, 2001).
4. *The Moon-god Allah in the Archeology of the Middle East* (Eugene, Oreg.: Harvest House, 1992), 8.
5. James Rudin, "The Vocabulary of Terrorism" Religion News Service (October 11, 2001).
6. Quoted in *El Mundo* (Caracas, Venezuela, February 1980).
7. Barbara Richmond, "Some facts about Islam." On the World Wide Web at: http://www.foryourglory.org/Islam.
8. "Algeria denies blame for massacres" BBC News, January 7, 1998. On the World Wide Web at: http://news6.thdo.bbc.co.uk/hi/english/world/newsid_45000/45439.stm.
9. Kenneth R. Timmerman, "Will Bush Stop Sudan Genocide?" *Insight Magazine*, June 25, 2001.
10. "Public executions and amputations on increase" Amnesty International News Service Press Release, May 21, 1998.
11. *Washington Post*, August 23, 1998.
12. "*Jihad* Against Jews and Crusaders" World Islamic Front Statement, February 23, 1998.
13. *Time* (December 23, 1998).
14. Albayan (May 12, 2001). Cited in a report by the Israeli Foreign Ministry, found on the World Wide Web at: http://www.likud.nl/extr111.html.

15. Al Iyyam (May 6, 2001). Ibid.
16. "Poll: 80% of Palestinians support suicide bombings," Associated Press, August 28, 2001.
17. Dr. Eyad Sarraj, "Why We Have Become Suicide Bombers" found on the World Wide Web at: http://www.missionislam.com/islam/conissue/palestine.htm.
18. Norman Doidge, "The Palestinians' little bombers: School textbooks teach children to admire the martyr." *National Post* (November 9, 2000).
19. Ibid.
20. Jack Kelley, "Devotion, desire drive youths to 'martyrdom,'" *USA Today* (August 5, 2001).
21. Some Islamic sources say Mohammed was *betrothed* to Aisha when she was six and the marriage was consummated when she was nine years old. In any case, it is clear that he married a child who was too young for marriage. It was an act of pedophilia. See Abu Iman 'Abd ar-Rahman, "The Young Marriage of 'Aishah" at: http://faridi.net/islam/aisha/.
22. Jack Kelley, "Devotion, desire drive youths to 'martyrdom,'" *USA Today* (August 5, 2001).
23. Charles Krauthammer, "Mideast Violence: The Only Way Out" *Washington Post* (August 16, 2001).
24. Ibid.
25. Cited in Mona Charen, "Reality check," *Jewish World Review* (August 17, 2001).
26. Aluma Solnick, "Martyrs & Mothers," found on the World Wide Web at: http://aish.com/jewishissues/middleeast/Martyrs_and_Mothers.asp

Chapter Three

1. John Piper, "On the Calamity in New York" at the *Banner of Truth* Web site: http://www.banneroftruth.co.uk/articles piper_on_the_calamity_in_new_york.htm.

Chapter Four

1. All but someone with a perverted sense of justice would agree that Nazi Germany, many communist governments, and other abusive dictatorships are evil. Yet *any* government is better than *no* government. Anarchy is deadly and chaotic for all.